T0311502

Cambridge Elements ⁼

Elements in Critical Issues in Teacher Education
edited by
Tony Loughland
University of New South Wales
Andy Gao
University of New South Wales
Hoa T. M. Nguyen
University of New South Wales

RECLAIMING THE CULTURAL POLITICS OF TEACHING AND LEARNING

Skooled in Punk

Greg Vass
Griffith University

CAMBRIDGE
UNIVERSITY PRESS

Shaftesbury Road, Cambridge CB2 8EA, United Kingdom

One Liberty Plaza, 20th Floor, New York, NY 10006, USA

477 Williamstown Road, Port Melbourne, VIC 3207, Australia

314–321, 3rd Floor, Plot 3, Splendor Forum, Jasola District Centre,
New Delhi – 110025, India

103 Penang Road, #05-06/07, Visioncrest Commercial, Singapore 238467

Cambridge University Press is part of Cambridge University Press & Assessment,
a department of the University of Cambridge.

We share the University's mission to contribute to society through the pursuit of
education, learning and research at the highest international levels of excellence.

www.cambridge.org
Information on this title: www.cambridge.org/9781009494519

DOI: 10.1017/9781009303460

First published 2024

A catalogue record for this publication is available from the British Library.

ISBN 978-1-009-49451-9 Hardback
ISBN 978-1-009-30348-4 Paperback
ISSN 2755-1202 (online)
ISSN 2755-1199 (print)

Reclaiming the Cultural Politics of Teaching and Learning

Skooled in Punk

Elements in Critical Issues in Teacher Education

DOI: 10.1017/9781009303460
First published online: May 2024

Greg Vass
Griffith University

Author for correspondence: Greg Vass, g.vass@griffith.edu.au

Abstract: Despite often being associated with anti-establishment, irreverent, and a do-it-yourself (DIY) rejection of dominant culture, less considered may the collaborative, communal, and curative threads of punk thinking, being, and doing. From the outset, punk offered critiques and alternative ways of conceptualizing a world and ways of worlding that are not as harmful and constraining as those encountered by many in the dominant milieu of life. This Element is focused on how and why punk can productively contribute to efforts that are responding to the influences of dominant culture in education, such as the effects of standardization, heightened accountabilities, and 'gap talk'. For this Element, punk can be thought of as social practices that generate cultural resources that can be utilized to critique the dominant culture. Hence, this Element aims to make the case that punk sensibilities offer educators opportunities to reclaim the cultural politics of teaching and learning.

Keywords: punk, teacher education, social justice, teacher/learner Identities, cultural politics of schooling

ISBNs: 9781009494519 (HB), 9781009303484 (PB), 9781009303460 (OC)
ISSNs: 2755-1202 (online), 2755-1199 (print)

Contents

1 The Learner in Schooling and Punk Lessons

1.1 'Take It or Leave It'

In this Element, I explore the possibilities that open up by working with punk in the context of schooling. Punk in this usage should not bring to mind notions of spiked hair, ripped clothes, and anti-authoritarian rage, though it can gesture in these directions. Instead of this mental image, the approach to punk taken up here should evoke a sense of resisting corporatocracy, drawing attention to unpalatable (or actively harmful) sociopolitical practices, a sense of community that fosters individuality, and a commitment to rolling up your sleeves to get things done – rather than waiting around for things to get done by others. This conceptualization draws on ideas from Way (2021, p. 108), who explores punk as being a 'state of mind' underpinned by a set of 'core values', an understanding which is being reworked for this Element in terms of punk sensibilities.[1]

In this section you will be introduced to the topics connected with schooling that are of central interest to the Element. This starts with looking at why identities matter in education. This is of course a key touchstone of teacher education; however, the aim is to (re)consider learner identities and why they matter when explored with punk sensibilities, an undertaking that highlights some of the complexities linked with identity-work during the school years. Following this, attention turns to the broader classroom environment to (re)consider this setting in terms of communities of learners, as read through punk sensibilities, which aims to push beyond rudimentary notions of learning as a social endeavour. This leads to the part of the section that advocates for wider take-up of punk sensibilities in schooling, and specifically this is explored through consideration of the 'do-it-yourself' (DIY) approach, which offers a reminder of the agency and capacity of educators to be local and low budget for teaching and learning.

Given that attention will turn to exploring concerns to do with identities, it may be helpful to offer a few comments about me and my connections with punk. This is also 'proper' in the spirit of punk community-making and the approach to crafting this text. As Dines (2015b, p. 131) asserts, for 'punk scholarship' to be read and engaged with as meaningful and rigorous, 'it needs to be self-critical, reflective, and at times, self-deprecating'.[2] Moreover, it is simply good academic practice to be critically reflexive, which in terms of methodology can be linked with autoethnography (p. 130). With a view to this, the first thing may be to note that if you asked me at any stage over the last thirty

---

[1] From Fat on the album *My Parents Like Me Now* (1993), Emily Records.
[2] Section 2 elaborates on the contestations that circulate in connection with defining punk and the conceptualization of punk sensibilities.

years if I would describe myself as punk, I would have been quick to say no. This is for a variety of reasons which hopefully will become clear later on.

However, thirty years ago my friends and I would regularly make the thirty or so minute walk from our share house on the outskirts of what is affectionately referred to as the Valley in Meanjin[3] (Brisbane, Australia) to see bands. In the lead up to 1993 this included bands such as Fat playing songs such as 'Take it or leave it' (see subheading 1.1). Over the years, I have described the experience of seeing Fat like having electricity plugged into my spine. They had a huge sound that hit you like a wall. There was an anger in their performances that was impossible to miss. They were political. The energy was frenetic and highly charged from start to finish. It was an experience to be in a venue with them and was like nothing else I had ever encountered – which isn't really saying that much, given I grew up in a household without music. My recollections of music from early childhood were my mother's love of classic 1950s and 1960s musicals, which was a hangover from her own youth growing up in a children's home in the suburbs of Brisbane. It was my older sister who initially brought music into the household, but the one-hit-wonders that dominated the mid-1980s were equally unremarkable in terms of impact.

Live music was transformative – and not just aesthetically or aurally. It was everything that was part and parcel of moving out of home, not having much money, share housing, attending venues that were rough around the edges, and listening to non-commercial bands. Also, this was all located within a broader social milieu that offered the promise of opportunity, wealth, and social climbing as part of marketing mainstream culture and politics. Brisbane was very keen at the time, and continues to make bold claims, of being a global city. The inequities, excess, and exclusion that were increasingly evident to me in my day-to-day life were jarring. This was a time when ideas, artefacts, and the politics of punk were helping me to make sense of myself and the worlds I was moving through. But at the time and in the years since, I did not think of myself as punk per se. However, on reflection, a sense of punk has stayed with me over the decades, informing my views of the world and actions within it, and hence the notion of punk sensibilities resonates as a way of describing this. So, as you work through the text, you can *take it or leave it* in terms of thinking about whether or not I am punk enough to be writing this text, but don't let that get in the way of thinking about what punk has to offer education.

1.2 Why Learner Identities Matter

There are a couple of driving motivations underpinning this Element. The first is to do with *identities* in schooling – the learner, the teacher, and other people that

---

[3] See www.turrbal.com.au/ for more about the local people prior to and since invasion.

potentially impact on schooling. And linked with this, the second is to do with the potential role that *punk sensibilities* may offer educators who have the sort of curricular and pedagogical chutzpah that enables them to engage with learners in ways that may improve schooling experiences for many. Part of my reasoning, which is likely not too dissimilar to what many other educators experience, are those encounters in schooling that stick with us long after they have occurred. They are instances that can raise questions, leave us feeling unsettled, or serve as a reminder of the inadequacies of the institutional machinery we have become a part of. Maybe a couple of examples might help with thinking a little further in this direction.

The first of these comes from when I was still a newly minted high school teacher in suburban Brisbane – nearly twenty years ago. From early in the school year, I observed that one of my year nine students would regularly sleep through the weekly lesson we shared in first period. This was a student that colleagues had cautioned me about having on my class roll, at the end of the previous year. And true to this predicted form, when he wasn't sleeping, curbing the potential for him to disrupt teaching and learning seemed beyond my skill set at the time. Letting him sleep, if that is what he chose to do, seemed the course of least resistance and enabled the class to cover territory that may have been more challenging in social science lessons than if he was awake.

As the first term turned into the second it seemed that confrontations with him started to subside, and in an unexpected turn of events – out of earshot of other students – he shared something with me about his life. Both his parents were shift workers, and as the eldest, on school days he was required to run the household morning routine with his younger siblings. This typically entailed getting them up, cleaned, fed, and out the door to school – and by extension, himself, then off to school. On these occasions his day would start early, and by 9.30 am he was ready for a rest. He also was of the view that as he contributed to the world in adult-like ways, why did those in school continue to insist on treating him like a troubled and troubling child. I have always thought it was a fair point to make.

To me, this was not the sort of story that I expected to hear, given the dominant voices in the school insisting he did not value education. It was also the sort of explanation that put into relief his sleeping of a morning and helped shed a different light on disruptive behaviour when he wasn't. At the time I questioned why his story wasn't better understood. Or if it was, why it wasn't shared in ways that led to more constructive outcomes in school for him. The brief chats that I did have with colleagues, such as the year level co-ordinator, were responded to with a shrug and the suggestion there was not much that could be done. But I wondered what an educator can or should do with this sort of insight once they know about it. And I also wondered about the perspective and experience of the student. Did he expect that teachers would already know his situation and change their behaviour? Did he hope that teachers wouldn't know about it? Why did he decide to share this snippet about his personal life with me?

In the end, I let him sleep through the first period lessons, encounters regarding behaviour and interruptions continued to reduce, and he did enough to pass. But at the end of the year, I was left with questions that continue to echo through my thinking. Prominent amongst these being, if this was in any way indicative of his formal educational experiences, what did he really learn in or from schooling that would help him later in life? What did he learn about himself and the world around him? And should schooling have offered him something more than this?

Another encounter, albeit at more of a distance, was closer to the end of my time as a high school educator. In this instance, the recent arrival of a senior student mid-term generated a swell of gossip amongst the staff. To be clear, at no stage did I meet the student in person, but this didn't change the fact that details about his life were shared between staff during brief encounters around the school. The couple of times I did catch sight of him, he was wearing a range of facial rings and a heavy duffle coat – despite the heat and humidity, and both of which were not school uniform. He was tall and imposing, with hands on hips; you were left with the impression that he maintained a permanent scowl. He looked every bit like a fish out of water in an otherwise generic suburban school. As the story went, our school had been pressured into taking him in, as he had been kicked out of all the high schools in his and the neighbouring catchment areas. We were a 'last resort'.

In the end, I don't think he lasted two weeks, not that I heard of any particular incidents that occurred involving him in that time. That was, until his final day. As chance would have it, the staffroom that I was located within bordered the school sports field, and one of my colleagues had observed the student mid-lesson sitting in the middle of the field smoking a cigarette, and subsequently called for the assistance of the school administration. That was the last that we heard or saw of the student. Again, I was left with questions that continue to float through my thinking. I am drawn to pondering: if this was indicative of his formal educational experiences, what did he really learn in or from schooling that would help him later in life? What did he learn about himself and the world around him? And should schooling have offered him something more?

A third and final vignette comes from my doctoral research, when I returned to the school where I had been a teacher to undertake a study about the ways that teaching and learning practices reproduce racialized meanings, and make race meaningful to those present (Vass, 2016, 2017). In the lead up to fieldwork, one of the deputy principals shared with me her interest regarding what the study might make of the high number of Aboriginal learners in the year eight cohort – there were nine students starting high school in this year level, which was considered significant for the white-washed bayside school.[4] At the time, this was the transition point from primary to secondary school, and as part of the handover process the information provided by the primary school educators had identified a number of these students as warranting careful attention in the high school. I am not sure who decided to subsequently put a number of these students together in the same class, and it is not worth speculating as to why. But I can say that the dynamics in the class did indeed make for a challenging teaching and learning environment.

To try and be clear, from my perspective at the time and to this day, I think it is problematic schooling practices that put what seemed to be a target on the backs of these students before they even walked through the school gate. In this sense, the problem was not, and never should be, ascribed to the learners or their backgrounds. As such, the deputy principal identifying this group of students and encouraging me to make sure that I observed lessons with them, was illustrative of the ways that schooling contributes to reproducing racialized identities and makes race meaningful in the lives of young learners. Hence, I would encourage pausing to think about what is and isn't possible for students to exert control and influence over, under circumstances such as this.

At the time, prominent positive classroom management practices encouraged deploying strategies designed to enable/force students to take responsibility for their behaviour (Mooney et al., 2008). And, up to a point, it is hard to disagree with the suggestion to use calm and consistent messaging to try and de-escalate the emotions that come up in the midst of classroom contestations, with a view to then reasserting a focus on teaching and learning. However, educators would do well to consider the point that many students are aware of (for example) racialized stereotypes or deficit assumptions, and of how these are attached to some students and not to others. Moreover, it is all too often evident to students where they are positioned within these racialized hierarchies. I would suggest that this was the case for many of the incoming year eight Aboriginal students. This, then, begs the questions, what can or should they do in conditions such as this?

Art was one of the classrooms I observed with this group. These lessons were practical (rather than theory or text based), with students invited to set them-selves up and work on upcoming assessment. During observations, one of the tasks focused on producing artworks that demonstrated tessellations being put

---

[4] In the Australian context, the terms Aboriginal and/or Torres Strait Islander, Indigenous, and First Nations are typically used in connection with schooling policies and practices. However, these terms are contested, given their foundations in the ongoing colonial occupation of unceded lands.

to work. More often than not, within minutes of the lesson starting the teacher would have a line-up of students at the front desk seeking individual assistance, with the remainder of the class then entertaining themselves. In short, there was a lot going on in the room, but not much of it had to do with tessellations.

I was uncomfortable at times observing, and this was not lost on the students who tried to draw me into exchanges. They were curious about my presence, my task of observing with pen and paper in hand, and perhaps with my decisions not to intervene with behaviour management. And it was indeed the case that some of the Aboriginal students were prominent with leading the disruptive behaviour, but they were far from alone. It was also evident that many of the students were familiar with each other, having shared much of their primary years of education. Some of the confrontations drew on this familiarity, or perhaps something that happened on the weekend. At times it was seemingly impossible to implement the responsible behaviour management strategies. Simply put, the consequences and implications for poor behaviour choices were not of immediate concern.

The teacher, who had willingly put his hand up to participate in the study, genuinely wanted to better understand and learn to foster pedagogical skills to work more effectively with classes such as this. However, it was still relatively early in his career. Art was afforded three 45-minute lessons a fortnight for twenty weeks, and accepting for interruptions such as public holidays and sport, this may result in as little as thirteen or fourteen hours contact time. How was he going to find the time to get to know the students and how they learn in meaningful ways? What sorts of strategies would work for this undertaking? Are genuine teacher–student relationships achievable under such circumstances?

As with the other examples, the memory of observing these lessons left me with questions that have defied simple or quick explanations. Again, I wonder if this was in any way indicative of the formal educational experiences of students in the class; what might be learnt in or from schooling that helps them later in life? What do students learn about themselves and the worlds they walk through under such circumstances? And should schooling offer something more than this?

As has hopefully been illustrated by these vignettes, the identities and identity-work of students matters. The sense of self, the relationship with education (in an abstract sense), and teachers (in a day-to-day sense), and the constraints imposed by – or at least intertwined with – societal forces, converge in complex and at times overwhelming ways (Hall, 2000 – see also Collins & Bilge, 2016; Elliot, 2016; Lesko, 2012). These identity issues make school life hard for students and teachers, albeit for different reasons, and in ways that are experienced very differently. More than this, though, it is hoped that the vignettes also open up lines of questioning that resonate and draw attention to failings or limitations of the mainstream education system.

The desire for quick and easy solutions runs the risk of deflecting attention from schooling arrangements and practices. One form of this propensity for 'easy' interpretations that can be heard on occasion is the suggestion that formal education settings are not a good fit for some students, perhaps such as those in these vignettes. Or, as one of the science teachers at the school was fond of saying, students such as this need to meet teachers halfway by 'bringing something to the table' (Vass, 2017). But don't these sorts of utterances shift most – if not all – of the responsibility onto the learners? If the choices and behaviour of students and their backgrounds are established as the root of the 'problem' within schooling, what are educators 'bringing to the table'?

To me it sounds a lot like a deficit line of reasoning. And, as it struck me then – and still does – the potential remedies for this seem overly reliant on narratives about students who find that one special educator to connect with. It is the exception and the exceptional teacher that is all too often positioned as making the difference for some students in terms of nursing them through the system rather than them ending up being spat out by it. The heroic or saviour educator that has been popularized in film may come to mind here (Brown, 2015).

Reflecting on the vignettes and others like them from across my years in education, it seems that it is schooling that gives up on – or never really welcomed – some students. Additionally, I don't need to delve too far into details about the lives of the learners for you to get a sense of the complex interplay between the personal, the societal, and the institutional. Nor are these stories that can be helpfully unpacked through the lens of class (or socioeconomic status more broadly), race, gender, or any other isolated identity marker. There is an interaction at play that needs to be better understood and accounted for, and the term *intersectionality* has increasingly been utilized as an analytical tool that can assist with revealing the complexities of the identity-work and social worlds people move through (Collins & Bilge, 2016). The term *intersectionality*, first coined by Crenshaw (1991, p. 1245), sought to highlight 'the need to account for multiple grounds of identity when considering how the social world is constructed'.

To help move our thinking further in this direction, Au (2012, p. 61) offers the reminder that it is the intersecting influences of multiple social locations that we all experience which are fundamental to how we 'know' the worlds we live within and move through. Said another way, socially and politically generated ideas about class, gender, and race (for example) rub up against each other in ways that are internalized. This is a process that shapes how we narrate our sense of self, but simultaneously this is enmeshed with how we story our relationships to and with others. These intersecting social locations have been described in terms of being our *standpoint*, a conceptualization that is simultaneously both individual and collective.

For Collins and Bilge (2016, p. 82), the more popularized or familiar conceptualization of intersectionality is intertwined with a *standpoint epistemology* – in other words, they are both concerned with the construction of knowledges. In common and pertinent to this discussion, intersectionality and standpoint theorizing are concepts that draw attention to the idea that it is the social locations of the oppressed which reveal the most about society-wide power relationships, and from this, the knowledge-making processes and arrangements that work to preserve the status quo (Au, 2012; Collins & Bilge, 2016).

Has it been too long since we have had a sentence with the word punk in it? Well, I am of the view that punk sensibilities may help some of us in our efforts with meaningfully getting to know and understand learners in ways that extend beyond academic achievement. In the three vignettes, it is not as if putting the blinkers on to hone in on academic achievement was likely to contribute to positive or more encouraging schooling experiences for the students. It is also not likely that some sort of curriculum-based response on its own would have resulted in improved outcomes. Something more or different was required. Now please don't misunderstand my intentions; I am not suggesting that we don't *ever* think about the academic part of schooling. But there is more to schooling than this.

If we return to consider Way's (2021) four punk values, they are helpful with thinking about the rhetorical questions asked above. The values she refers to include engaging with DIY approaches, being subversive, fostering political consciousness, and sustaining community practices. For instance, is it possible to imagine that those in formal educational settings, such as the suburban high school from the vignettes, are willing and able to establish and maintain a sense of community that would have enabled more positive outcomes? Well, why not? In each of the stories, the students were arriving at the school gate with first-hand knowledge and experiences of the structural arrangements that they were in the midst of. More than this, though, they had established skills and strategies that helped them navigate this system, but perhaps not with the strategies and sense of community to envisage pathways to effect changes to the structural arrangements as such. Isn't this where educators can and should create learning environments that value and work with the knowledges and skills that students arrive with, and from this enable them to positively change the worlds they are moving through or into?

Next, were there potential pathways that could have allowed for the subversive inclinations that permeate through the vignettes to be redirected in productive and generative ways, rather than having educators try to contain what were viewed as disruptive responses to schooling? Why not here too? If educators (and I would include myself) had worked with students to positively channel subversive dispositions and ways of acting on and in the world, perhaps schooling would have been experienced as something positive, instead of being something to endure or escape from. And yes, in each of the vignettes the students were already being subversive up to a point. The onus is therefore directed more at educators to find ways to resist and reimagine schooling environments which actively embrace, value, and work with the energy and effort it takes for students that have been labelled as 'disengaged', 'unmotivated', or 'disruptive', in order that they may maintain these facets of their identities while also redirecting them in some form.

Moreover, fostering this sort of subversive disobedience would likely be part and parcel of developing the sort of sociopolitical consciousness that may have empowered the students in ways that later enabled them to continue exerting influence on and in the world beyond the school gate. However, in order that these sorts of sensibilities may surface in ways that students experience meaningfully, it seems that educators must commit to, and enact, a DIY approach to getting things done in ways that interrupt the status quo of mainstream schooling. And there is widespread agreement from those who advocate punk sensibilities as being in some way reliant on this DIY ethos and activity (see Parkinson, 2018; Santos & Guerra, 2018; Woods, 2021).

1.3 Communities of Learners

The notion of establishing communities of learners as an important touchstone for educational practices is far from new or innovative. Texts about teaching and learning are full of stories, theory, and empirical evidence that encourage educators to find ways of meaningfully taking up sociocultural approaches in the classroom (see McInerney, Walker & Liem, 2011). Messaging often runs along the lines of learning being a social process (Lee et al., 2020). We learn from and with each other. The context matters. Learners benefit from scaffolding that connects with what they already know, has relevance for them, and extends them in ways that enable growth – by better understanding what they don't know or do well (Webster & Ryan, 2019, p. 202).

In my experience, these sorts of ideas continue to have currency and are observable. For example, through suggestions such as mixed ability groups providing scope for high achievers to be extended, while assisting to elevate the achievements of lower-achieving students. This typically occurs within classes, however, there are also between-class ability groupings (also known as streaming), which remains common despite the evidence that seeks to debunk the assumed benefits of this practice (Francis, Taylor & Tereshchenko, 2020). For instance, numerous international studies have compared the impact associated with mixed ability grouping practices in schooling and have shown they are more likely to result in lowering academic achievements overall, rather than raising these (Scarlett, 2015, p. 2). Of additional worry, studies from the OECD (the Organisation for Economic Co-operation and Development) indicate that grouping practices in schooling can serve to increase achievement gaps based on socioeconomic status (Scarlett, 2015, p. 2 – see also Johnston & Taylor, 2023).

Do we – as educators – think long and hard enough about the logic and evidence in connection with the benefits of group work? Moreover, do we pause to consider in depth or detail the ways that the world has changed since the foundations of sociocultural theories were established by the likes of Vygotsky in post-revolution Russia, or started being popularized more widely from the 1970s (McInerney et al., 2011)? A time linked with the emergence of what is loosely referred to as neoliberalism, a term describing the agenda, institutional arrangements, and practices focused on 'economic and social transformation under the sign of the free market' (Connell, 2013, p. 100). Speaking to the circumstances in Australia, though I suspect of relevance to many settings, Reid (2020) outlines a case regarding the deleterious consequences now evident from more than thirty years of neoliberalism shaping schooling, calling for an 'alternative and coherent narrative' that challenges these effects as urgently required.

For many of the educators that I work with, sociocultural learning is linked with groupwork and creating communities of learners, and is understood as being a key strategy that demonstrates a form of differentiation (Tomlinson, 2017).[5] Though it may not have been intentional, the logic of sociocultural learning in this form often relies on assumptions about the learning benefits of differentiating, such as improved academic achievements for mixed-ability groupings. Or the teacher could strategically place the fast or more able writers with those who are not; those students that are more likely to have completed homework with those that may not, and so on. An example of how the assumed merits of groupwork can play out in higher education may be the more banal hope that at least one person in a group has engaged with the set reading. In my experience, as with the other examples of mixed ability groupings, the actual learning benefits are hit and miss at best.

Another expression that espouses the merits of creating communities of learners is underpinned by belief in the benefits of creating 'safe' learning

---

[5] It may be an unhelpful distraction to start unpacking what is meant by differentiation here. The very short-hand version is to think of it as an umbrella term linked with 'inclusion', which refers to a host of ideas and practices that aim to respond to concerns that impact on student learning. A recent paper from Gibbs and McKay (2021) highlights that it is a term with conceptual and applied confusion that requires more considered and careful scrutiny.

environments (Tomlinson, 2017). Without wanting to state the obvious, creating unsafe spaces in which effective teaching and learning takes place is clearly absurd. It seems unimaginable that an educator would suggest anything other than a desire for all students to be respectful of their own learning and that of others. But again, this is far from straightforward. Illustrative of this, in recent years I have observed and heard stories about students offering critiques or commentary that may be experienced as a form violence by others, and then defending their position with claims to 'free speech'. In this way, a community of learners is presented with heated and challenging encounters when racist, sexist, homophobic, sacrilegious, or other discriminatory and/or offensive views are shared and then defended. The personal 'rights' of individuals (or a small group) are put forward as superseding the rights and interests of the learning community. To be sure, these are teachable moments in many respects, but finding ways to effectively do so remains challenging (Zembylas, 2020).

As is gestured to by these lines of thinking, across my time as an educator I have grown increasingly wary about the emphasis that seems to locate the reasoning in support of social learning practices as benefitting the individual. In other words, the merits placed on this approach – more often than not – are put forward as strategies that assist individual learners in some form. For example, the learning experienced via interacting with others may improve the academic achievements of individuals – and when it doesn't go this way, such as the perception of dragging down the achievements for some during groupwork, the teacher is informed of this swiftly. It is readily imaginable that most of you have a story or two to share about the challenges that are part and parcel of grading group assessment! Rather than relying on the assumed benefits of groupwork and learning as a social practice, perhaps it is the growing influence of neoliberal thinking across the sector that more usefully sheds light on the emphasis placed on individualism, even within a context calling for the benefits of learning socially.

There are tensions between the rights and benefits for individuals when considered alongside the social good and benefit for communities that seem to cast a long shadow over education nowadays. For instance, it may be that fostering communities of learners strengthens the communication and collaborative skills of those involved. This was illustrated in the research that informed the development of the *productive pedagogies* framework, as the working with and valuing difference elements were grounded in observable practices to do with creating and maintaining learning communities that are collaborative and supportive, which was intertwined with deep listening in the form of narratives and valuing cultural knowledges (Hayes et al., 2006, pp. 68–69). An important premise in this sense, as encouraged by the productive pedagogies framework, is learning how to genuinely listen to others, be active contributors, compromise, problem solve, and so on. And educators can't assume that students arrive with these skills and knowledges; hence, they need to be explicitly taught.

Again, few would likely disagree with the importance of providing opportunities for students to actively practice and improve these interpersonal knowledges and skills. However, is there time in an already busy and congested curriculum environment with increasing accountabilities to do so, and do so well? Moreover, the policy and curricular rationale underpinning the emphasis of these sorts of knowledges and skills is largely premised on the notion that these are transferable capabilities to be of use later in life – they help the learner as they enter and compete in the world of paid employment (Webster & Ryan, 2019). In view of this, there is a danger that the good intentions and benefits of learning socially have been recast as of benefit largely to the individual, which is part and parcel of the broader neoliberal imaginary in which 'human beings are configured as human capital across all spheres of life' (Rizvi, 2022, p. 221).

It may seem to some of you that this is a somewhat pedantic or semantic line of concern to be raising. So, I should offer another caveat and move on by noting that for me, there has long been something a little unsettling about offering reasoning for articulating support for, and initiating activities grounded by the notion that learning is a social undertaking, when the outcomes are largely motivated by individual gains. I find much to agree with in the ideas outlined by Lesko (2012), who makes a compelling case regarding the intensification of competition, particularly in secondary schooling, as having harmful consequences for many learners in formal educational settings. She argues that 'enhanced competition of fast-tracked capital and the replacement of welfare supports with demands for self-sufficiency have begun to effect changes to students' relations, in the politics of secondary schooling, and in the enhanced rigor of schools being promoted through high-stakes testing' (p. 173). In essence, the hypervisibility of intensified competition has reduced the variety and scope of social locations available to students, and this is compounded by what Lesko describes as 'poisonous pedagogies' (p. 177).[6]

In contrast with this, establishing a community of learners by drawing on punk sensibilities moves in a very different direction. It is less about individual reward and competition, and instead places emphasis on concerns to do with

---

[6] Lesko concludes her chapter with this expression, but it is not elaborated on. The passage from Lesko reads as follows: 'As socioeconomic pressures accelerate competition, adolescents in school are bombarded with prerequisites for them to be valued by others and by themselves. Unfortunately, schools are largely conducting business as usual, distracted by high-stakes testing, and with little attention or resources devoted to peer group dynamics, intolerance, harassment, and other forms of "poisonous pedagogies".'

well-being by enabling individuals to find their place within the social group, or where the shared efforts of those pulling in a similar direction are enhanced. This is not put forward to romanticize or simplify the suggestion. To be sure, there will be disputes, differences, and contestations within and across punk-influenced classrooms. The family analogy may be useful here to help illustrate this point (see Kwiatek, 2022); for example, there are clearly differences along with similarities that could be observed if you sat down to a family meal with my brother, sisters, and myself. It is also likely the case that my parents did not want any of us – as individuals – to be more successful than any of the others in the family, nor did they seemingly go out of their way to favour one sibling more than the others, though if you asked my siblings they may disagree with this! But this is okay too, as it gestures to the point that maybe there is more to the notion of communities of learners that can be considered.

Ruminations from Santos and Guerra (2018) may be helpful here, as they grapple with the notion that punk sensibilities open up pathways to support the identity-work of young people through a shared resistance and dissent to reproduction of the dominant culture. Dines (2015a) also discusses similar lines of thinking, referring to the intertwining of intellectual engagement with empowerment and social responsibility. As he explains, it is the 'porous nature of punk' that enables people to draw on a diverse array of resources in their efforts to restory their identities and create meaning in the lives of others and themselves (p. 22). Parkinson (2018, p. 187) is somewhat more direct when noting that the identity-work of learners is central to their learning experiences, with punk potentially serving as an 'ethical, epistemological and aesthetic resource for participants . . . in their resistance to a perceived status quo'. In the way I think of this, the emphasis moves away from efforts to outlast, outperform, or outshine those within our community of learners, which as Lesko (2012) suggests, may be offered as characterizing the dominant culture in schooling. Instead, we could and should initiate schooling practices that are genuinely supportive, and exert collective effort to push back on the hegemonic forces that seek to put us in competition with each other.

An example of punk sensibilities putting this approach into action may be observed in the Riot Grrrl scene. While this scene may have foundations that are typically associated with the US, the intertwining of punk and feminist expressions of empowerment were evident from the outset and wherever punk was emerging (Karpp, 2019). While it is indeed abundantly clear that 'a roster of women artists seized punk by the throat' from the outset (Nguyen, 2012, p. 174), the Riot Grrrl 'revolution' arguably provided a form of visibility that culminated in the scene having a global presence that is 'part of a borderless community of feminist agents seeking to make gender and gender bodies visible on their own terms, while also insisting on an awareness of local/national political and social contexts' (Dunn, 2016, p. 116). For Lusty (2017, p. 220), gesturing in this sort of direction may benefit from a cautious acknowledgement regarding concerns that the Riot Grrrl movement was 'co-opted by narcissistic populism and commercial culture'.

Despite this caution, Lusty (2017) encourages revisiting contributions to the movement such as the manifestos that were circulated through zines in collective consciousness-raising efforts in support of a 'highly flexible and mobile political subject for whom the discourse of revolution and civil disobedience signals both a collective fantasising and a disruptive public identity' (p. 226). The production, distribution, and engagement with zines were not only illustrative of the DIY ethic, they also were pedagogical, sharing insights regarding why there are good reasons for collective agency to interrupt the structural arrangements that underpin the reproduction of patriarchy and heteronormativity (for instance), and there are diverse ways that everybody can – and should – contribute to feminist politics. The zines were augmented not only by the recordings and performances of artists; the Riot Grrrl movement established networks that enabled 'elders' in the scene to teach and model feminist literacy skills (Cordova, 2017, p. 35).

Schilt and Giffort (2012) also note that punk has long been a 'girl-centred' subcultural milieu in which intergenerational connections between younger and older punks were a touchstone for furthering broader feminist agendas. They investigated the organization and running of not-for-profit 'band camps' that not only worked towards making punk more accessible to a wider audience, but they also focused on the empowerment and agency of women in society more broadly. The band camps were clearly understood as addressing a broader political framework that sought to foster the sorts of skills and knowledges that would enable acting on and in the world in ways that interrupt the dominant structural arrangements (Schilt & Giffort, 2012, p. 152). There is a shared collective goal – which I find the intertwined concepts from Dale (2016, p. 1) that focus on *empowerment* and *novelty* useful – that is expansive enough for everybody to have a role to contribute. In this sense, there is solidarity and agency when engaging with teaching and learning activities that push back and interrupt the ongoing dominance of patriarchal structural arrangements and thinking.

1.4 A DIY Approach to Interrupt Standardizing Practices

It seems to me that efforts to establish communities of learners that resonate with the ideas just outlined – instead of deriving from competition and individuality – require the meaningful take-up of DIY approaches to schooling. In a way, as with

Beer's (2014) musings about the riskiness and truncated efforts of (punk) sociologists to be bold and inventive in the face of being trained to conform and preserve the comprehensibility of the field, so too must educators find ways to actively resist and push back on what teaching and learning has become in the period of hyperaccountabilities. For my part, this Element could be described as an attempt to try to walk this talk. For instance, I have approached crafting the text in ways that some may view as academically unorthodox. At the least, this will become more apparent in the next section, and I hope that you persist and can see the potential merits of trying to interrupt dominant and normative conventions when it comes to writing about and for educators.

Relles and Clemens (2018, pp. 322–323) also encourage a DIY sensibility with academic scholarship, requiring a commitment to experimental modes of production and distribution, with the merits of these efforts determined by the active take-up of this output in ways that genuinely advance social justice agendas. Some may question this line of thinking – as one of the reviewers for the manuscript did – with a view to this text being published by an academic press and subsequently implicated in dominant marketing practices and copywriting rules. Fair point. This is a line of thinking that will be revisited later in connection with the challenge that is sometimes bandied about when someone is perceived as having 'sold out'.

The blurring of the personal and professional, the tensions and accommodations that are concomitant when balancing style or form with content and politics, as Dines (2015b) explores in some detail, are not easily negotiated. But I am also encouraged by the likes of Dunn (2023, p. 87) who talks about this in terms of 'mastering the tools of my trade but employing them in non-traditional ways . . . I'm going to use those tools to speak with intensity and focus on matters of extreme importance'. In view of these sorts of sentiments, it is my hope that the text does not wash over readers as simply another academic resource that they go through the motions of engaging with and is soon forgotten. Instead, in writing the Element as being a little personal, unorthodox, irreverent, direct, and blunt at times, I hope that it is engaging in ways that are memorable, provocative, and result in being proactive in future teaching and learning environments.

The distinction that Dunn (2016, p. 11) makes between commercial punk and DIY punk may be useful here, with the former being created and underpinned by logics and an ethos of being for profit, whereas the latter has a political agenda. With this in mind, from the outset the DIY ethos and practices have been a core facet of punk sensibilities. Also making note of this, Bennett and Guerra (2018) go on to outline how and why DIY punk has been transformed since the mid-1970s, with the most significant facet of this being the folding out of this ethos and practices to be one of lifestyle – the holistic distancing one can now pursue, 'from the institutional and cultural politics of neoliberal existence' (p. 14). To be honest, I am not entirely convinced about this yet, as it sounds like the other side of the coin in relation to the neoliberal-inspired entrepreneurial subject – the 'good citizen' that pursues self-interest and seemingly gives little regard to those forces that continue to exploit the environment and people for profit and personal gain (Kelly, 2006). However, I am open to the possibility of being convinced otherwise.

Instead, I am perhaps more inclined to work with the ideas from Relles and Clemens (2018) who move away from the idea that DIY sensibilities can help to create and maintain a parallel world, a type of *twilight zone* that operates independently of the dominant cultural milieu, and instead return our attention to the micro-politics of change that may be more accessible without venturing too far into the unknown. In this sense, our DIY efforts can be less concerned with scale or scope, and instead focus on the political in more localized ways. It is an approach that gestures to the ways that punk can be understood as a 'set of social activities', and these may not even directly relate to musical tastes and stylistic expressions (Dunn, 2016). Hence, it can be the micro or contextualized political actions that may directly – or in many cases indirectly – contribute to interrupting dominant cultural practices in ways that create spaces and opportunities for being and doing things that may not be characterized as revolutionary efforts to destroy the system, but nonetheless provide safe havens for other like-minded people.

An example of this from somebody close to me, namely, my primary school teacher wife, may help illustrate these lines of thinking. She decided to join the parents and community committee at our son's school and was somewhat surprised (and perhaps a little disappointed) to discover how few people were attending. So few, in fact, that she came home from one of the initial meetings having acquired the responsibility for organizing the upcoming Mother's Day stall. The first year our son attended this event, he had come home with a collection of cheap, plastic, imported trinkets. This is understandable on some levels – it is probably more convenient, likely makes more money for the school than other alternatives, and may even present the notion of choice in the eyes of the children attending. However, this sort of ode to the wonders of capitalism, free trade, and globalization seems a long way off from the sort of thing we remember doing ourselves as children at school. And given that my wife and I are both educators, we understand that time is precious and the curriculum is crowded, so shifting the responsibility on to educators to do something seemed unhelpful.

In the end, my wife decided to do something in her capacity of helping to plan for the stall, and for months prior to the event we cared for little succulent plants under our house. As a family, we had replanted a couple of hundred plants into little pots we bought, watered them, and then the day before the stall the plants were carefully wrapped, and both my son and daughter helped to make little happy Mother's Day messages that were stuck into each plant. She had done the math in terms of working out that in a school with little over 150 students, there were enough for each student to buy on average 1.5 plants. The little plants were $3 each, and the bigger ones $5. Close to the Mother's Day event, a few other people involved started expressing concerns about the variety and amount of things available. So they decided that in addition to the succulent pots, the left-over trinkets from the previous year would also be available. Interestingly, a few other people also heard what was happening, and they decided to contribute to the stall with home-made goods that would be cost-effective.

After the event, my wife reflected on some of the complications, such as those students that had come along with $50, who were unable to find enough things to purchase, and the other committee members' concerns that this may have been a missed opportunity to fund-raise more effectively. However, on balance, there seemed to be a positive reception, with feedback from students and parents appreciative of being able to participate in such a different event in comparison with what had become the norm. Not that this is the point of the story. Rather, despite my wife being unlikely to describe this as punk, I am drawn to thinking of this as putting to work a DIY punk sensibility. It was a social activity that made a localized political statement; it was an event that interrupted dominant capitalist practices of mass consumption. This is a story about not waiting for the world to change, but about being proactive and doing things on and in the world. The school Mother's Day stall offers a reminder that there are small everyday ways that practices can interrupt dominant schooling efforts that constrain and limit the work undertaken with learners, and there are positive and constructive reasons to pursue these activities.

1.5 You Learnt Three Chords? Then Form a Band!

Before reading any further, and despite the enthusiastic encouragement for punk to more widely influence schooling practices, it is perhaps worth noting that this Element should not be approached with the expectation that it will outline how anybody should or could enact punk sensibilities within educational settings. Instead, I hope to encourage a much deeper, sustained, and serious engagement with punk from those involved in education, and with how and why schooling is implicated within, reproduces, but can also serve to interrupt the dominant culture. For some, this is an ambition that may hold little interest. Fine. This text may not be for you.

But for others, particularly those who already have a sense of how and why the influences of dominant culture underpin why schooling may be an unwelcoming, unrewarding, and uninspiring place for many learners – this Element may be for you. Moreover, it may also be of interest to those of you who appreciate that this is concomitantly implicated in the reproduction of unearned or subconscious inclusion, privilege, and opportunity for other learners. Said another way, the students we encounter in school are already familiar in explicit and implicit ways with the dominant culture, so why not draw on materials that offer critical insights of dominant culture to ask interesting and engaging questions in the classroom?

Another point of consideration that warrants being touched on stems from concerns to do with the potential domestication of punk in formal school settings. The import of this is well worth holding onto across the remainder of this text, though more will be said in connection with this later. In short, if punk sensibilities are to be meaningfully engaged with in schooling, holding vigilantly onto the political underpinnings of the movement must be maintained. If punk is conceptualized in ways that are trivial and cursory, as entertaining hooks that capture the attention of learners prior to returning to business-as-usual teaching and learning, then very little will likely change. I am mindful here of the way that Torrez (2012) draws on the work of Illich to distinguish *schooling*, which entails being immersed within institutionalized settings in which socialization occurs, from *education*, which entails being immersed in knowledge-making practices.[7] It seems to me, as will be gestured to in Section 4, that schools emphasizing the former at the expense of the latter run the risk of actively contributing to the disengagement of some young learners from formal teaching and learning contexts.

It is with a view to this line of thinking that I would suggest that a shift in discursive apparatus may be helpful, and to riff from the work from Dines (2023) and his discussion about the skool bus movement in 1980s UK, perhaps a move towards the punk-inspired sense of *skooling* would be useful. Significant in this regard, as Dines points out, is reconceptualizing how teaching and learning can be framed and approached to 'fit the child', rather than expecting and enacting practices designed to shape the child in ways that 'fit the school' (p. 157). This is more than the semantics of language, it is about doing schooling differently if we want to produce different outcomes. For those learners who are unable or unwilling to 'fit in', those who push back, question, or challenge the pressures to 'fit in' in a variety of ways, an education is sought

---

[7] It may come as little surprise that Illich was writing in the early 1970s, which again highlights the concerns being shared during this period about changes that were impacting on schools, teaching, learning, and the experiences of students.

elsewhere, and as the research from Cordova (2017) highlights, for some this comes from punk. In my way of thinking, it is punk sensibilities which are urgently needed in schooling to help make the education on offer more relevant and valuable for many young learners. And if the punk is sanitized it is hardly likely to achieve this outcome.

With the aspiration of attempting to put punk sensibilities to work, the Element is not set out and framed in the same way that dominant forms of academic writing are structured or presented – though it is informed by and includes references to a wide collection of sources. As already evident, it will be a bit conversational. I will also add anecdotes that try to connect you with experiences and illustrate punk sensibilities at work, which will also hopefully help make the text a little more engaging than is sometimes the case with academic writing – though I can't promise that this is going to be the case for everybody. And, while it may be a struggle at times, I will endeavour to keep the writing short and to the point. In this way, hopefully the text will evoke the sense of being a collection of punk songs, which are often conceived – or at the least as they were in the early days of punk – as being a bit rough around the edges; short, loud, and irreverent. In this way, and like others before me, I am tempted to connect this with the iconic image that adorned the cover of a fanzine in the 1970s which depicted three chords and simply stated, 'now form a band' (cf. Beer, 2014, p. 20; Dale, 2016; Parkinson, 2018).

Wouldn't it be great if more teaching and learning were like this?!

2 A Kind of Punk Education

2.1 'White People Go to School, Where They Teach You How to Be Thick'[8]

In the previous section the central concerns to do with identities and social justice in education were introduced, and three intertwined punk sensibilities were offered as useful conceptual tools through which to reconsider schooling. This section will further develop these lines of thinking, but it will also delve more specifically into unpacking the activities and theory that sit behind the emergence of punk. To do so, the opening subsection offers a snapshot of the influence of standardizing practices and the increasing effects of accountabilities as they flow from teacher education into other areas of the educational landscape. For this, the notion of 'gracious submission' is introduced as it serves to illustrate how and why those of us in education may succumb to what Ball (2016) described as the 'terrors of performativity' and the concomitant

---

[8] From the song 'White Riot' (1977) by The Clash, lyrics retrieved 9 October 2023 from https://genius.com/The-clash-white-riot-lyrics.

difficulties with 'refusing neoliberalism'. Following this, attention turns to consider the production and expression of punk culture, which, as already noted, draws attention to the precarious, contested, and porous ways that punk is understood. With a view to this, it is worth reiterating – probably a few times – the point put forward by Dale (2016, p. 23), that 'punk, whatever it may be, is certainly *not* a style' (original emphasis). Lastly, the section turns to locating myself and the punk sensibilities and educational practices that I have – at times unwittingly – been party to.

For me, the lyrics from The Clash that open this section are pertinent as we move in this direction, as intertwined undercurrents that sit across the section deal with the ways that dominant schooling policies and practices seemingly set out deliberately to narrow the scope and depth of teaching and learning offered to many students. This reading of the lyrics is in agreement with Hounslow-Eyre (2023, p. 30), who points out that rather than being mistaken as a song about so-called 'white power', 'it is clear that for a multitude of reasons, extending beyond the confines of the public school system Strummer experienced, he maintained the view that the education system "dumbs down" students and in some sense does not meet learner's needs'.

Thinking more about this, I am drawn to the recent work from Cordova (2017, p. 136) who discusses this in terms of 'miseducative experiences' that interrupt or derail the understandings and confidence that learners may have of themselves. As she concludes, 'Perhaps our duty as educators is to dedicate our professional lives to consciously observe learners create their own educative desire paths, rather than force them to walk on the miseducative pavement' (p. 148). Hence, instead of accepting that schooling will continue to be a miseducative experience for many learners, I agree with the sentiments from Woods (2022) regarding the provocative potential for punk sensibilities to constructively draw attention to the colonial excesses that formal education is implicated within, and moreover, to also open pathways to do something about it.

2.2 'Gracious Submission' in the Era of Educational Accountabilities

When I initially stumbled across the expression 'gracious submission' in the revised edition of Pinar's (2019, p. 18) book on curriculum theorizing, I was struck by a recent experience in teacher education. In his text, Pinar (2019) draws attention to the ever-growing influence of 'what works' accountabilities in education, the businessification of schooling, and the deprofessionalizing of teaching and teacher education. Which in essence, is another and more pointed way of making note of facets of schooling that have been negatively impacted on by neoliberal thinking. For me, the notion of gracious submission is an invitation to reflect on the political and economic power and influence – the subjugation, as he puts it – that now dominates educational policies and practices in locations such as the US, but equally resonates for me in the Australian context.

A recent reminder of these influences came up at that time in the academic calendar when we prepare and submit course profiles for approval. This is typically a relatively smooth process when minor adjustments are made, such as updated due dates, revising a few words in task descriptions, changing reading lists, and so on. However, on this occasion, the approval was pushed back and the request was made to revise my course learning outcomes, to align them explicitly with the nationally mandated professional standards for teachers. The course was designed to provide preservice educators with opportunities to develop their knowledges and skills regarding evidence-informed approaches to schooling. There are well-reasoned dimensions to this, such as learning how to analyse student assessment data, behavioural reports, or medical information that has been documented, and to then formulate plans for teaching from this. This is necessary work for educators, and these teacher practices do fall under the umbrella of several Australian professional standards, so in part this is itself not a major concern. But the course was also clearly entangled with the broader 'what works' policy environment.

Therefore, in my view, this also requires utilizing critically informed theoretical tools that enable educators to understand the constraints and complications that are associated with this sort of undertaking. This is crucial in order to avoid the reproduction of deficit perspectives and practices that aim to 'fix' educational concerns linked with students viewed through one-dimensional categories to do with race, language, culture, or medical conditions such as ADHD and autism – to name just a few. This is not to suggest anything about the import of coming to know, understand, and of being able to work with a student's background; rather, the point is to consider individuals through an intersectional lens (as discussed earlier), with all the complexity and uncertainty that goes with this. Indeed, for me, it was the knowledge and ability to apply critical-thinking skills that were more important than the technical proficiencies that are emphasized by standardized teacher professional practices. As such, the course learning outcomes should make visible the distinction between critical and technical knowledge and skills, and emphasize the mandated professional standards which potentially deflect attention from this.

Initially, I thought that the request to change the learning outcomes may have been some sort of error or misunderstanding. However, after seeking clarification, it was reiterated to me that there should be clear lines of sight between the mandated national professional standards for teachers, and the learning outcomes, the assessment tasks, and the assessment criteria. This struck me as a curious request, and still not entirely convinced, I pushed back with what I thought was a reasonable point: the national professional standards are not – and should not be – a proxy for the teacher education curriculum. The standards were not designed to be the de facto curriculum, and designing the course profile in this way would run the risk of narrowing the scope of what the learners would anticipate encountering in the course. In essence, if the learning outcomes and assessment for the course are structured in this way, there is the potentially unhelpful danger that it is only the professional standards that the teacher education students will see as having value for their learning. The follow-on effects from this would be less than ideal once out in schools.

While I tried reiterating the point that it may be important that we prepare the teacher education students to meet the requirements of the professional standards, these were not 'the' curriculum. I was then asked, albeit not in these words, to graciously submit to the request and make the adjustments to the course profile. Which I did . . . but I then went about teaching the course the way it was previously designed as informed by critical sociology to ask questions about the education policy environment that the course was mired within. Perhaps this could be described as a form of *gracious subversion*, and is illustrative of the punk sensibility of being subversive as described by Way (2021).

The encounter gestures towards a web of concerns to do with formal schooling. This Element seeks to contribute to those voices already drawing attention to a growing array of evidence that indicates the current education policy environment is exacerbating disengagement from learning and growing inequities. For example, Cochran-Smith and colleagues (2018) were provoked into responding to teacher education reforms in the US that are guided by policies and practices underpinned by accountability initiatives that have actively eroded democratic values and goals. While mindful that those involved in schooling should of course be accountable, the research they report on was motivated by concerns to shed further light on the long-term effects and harm that may stem from the current policy environment. Hence, they put forward the notion for *reclaiming accountability* in teacher education by purposefully disentangling schooling from the influences of 'market ideology and the human capital paradigm', which serves to reproduce (if not actively increase) inequities within and across social milieus (Cochran-Smith et al., 2018, p. 5).

The call to push back on the role and influence of economics and state-controlled ideologies is far from new. Influential contributions from Michael Apple that reach back to the 1970s are illustrative of efforts to reinvigorate the activism and intellectual labour of educators as curriculum workers who are well placed to interrupt the harmful effects of schooling. As he put it at the time:

we can now begin to get a more thorough understanding of how institutions of cultural preservation and distribution like schools create and recreate forms of consciousness that enable social control to be maintained without the necessity of dominant groups having to resort to overt mechanisms of domination. (Apple, 2019, p. 3)

With a view to this, the story about my gracious submission/subversion and the course profile can be understood as grounded in educational changes that have been underway for at least the last fifty years, and they are not particular to the institution I am working within. Indeed, the 'problem of accountability' has been documented as influencing education in many settings around the world for some time (Cochran-Smith et al., 2018, p. 135). So, it was perhaps unsurprising that Michael Apple attended and gave a keynote lecture in 2017 at the Re-imagining Education for Democracy Summit (Riddle & Apple, 2019) on the outskirts of Meanjin (Brisbane), a conference that I also attended. The motivation underpinning the event was to bring together people who shared concerns regarding the 'increasing marketisation and corporatisation of education, as well as a commitment to the project of democratising education' (p. 4). The Summit included workshops, keynotes, presentations, and symposia designed to get participants thinking, talking, and creating a sense of community to carry them forward.

This event was a sort of call to arms to those who share the view that the role and contribution of schooling should be to offer critical education. However, for this to be realized, there must also be further ways opened up for educators to resist the pressures and constraints of gracious submission in the era of accountabilities. As Pinar (2019) gestures, the accountabilities era is fundamentally focused on controlling the *what* and *how* of teaching and learning by placing misguided emphasis on outcomes, 'despite the utter unpredictability of learning' (p. 19). Does punk offer an approach to schooling and further scope for acts of gracious subversion that exposes genuine alternatives that both work with and value the unpredictability of learning?

2.3 The Production, Expression, and Politics of Punk Culture

It may come as little surprise that the emergence of punk is linked with the economic, social, technological, and political shifts of the 1970s, and with prominent scenes such as those in New York and London – the likes of the Ramones and Sex Pistols likely come easily into the imaginary. However, the foundations of punk precede this time, and those exploring and playing with punk sensibilities were not constrained by, or only located within, male-dominated whitewashed English-speaking middle-class urban centres. For instance, Dunn (2016, p. 97) makes note of a plaque dedicated to Los Saicos in Lima (Peru) that claims to be the birthplace of punk in 1964. Habell-Pallán (2005) details the rise and impact of punk Chicanas in East Los Angeles in the 1970s. While Silva and Guerra (2019) unpack the emergence of punk in Portugal from the 1970s, Steward (2019) locates the 1979 Revolution in Iran as creating the roots of Iranian punk-infused 'do-it-yourself' cultural production, and punk would emerge in Indonesia (Donaghey & Prasetyo, 2021) and China (Xiao, 2019) a few years later. The widespread and rapid take up of punk is telling, and from the outset education was implicated in this. As observed by Schwartz (2015) in reference to the US in the 1970s, the influences of heightened accountabilities in education, the standardizing of schooling practices, and observable growing inequities were central to the formation of punk.

Given the varying contexts, times, and diversities of people involved, it is notoriously difficult and contentious to try and pin down what is (or isn't) punk. Furness (2012) discusses this:

> Through often conflicting accounts and histories of punk, one can identify the ebb and flow of countless scenes, interwoven subcultures and a broader 'Do it Yourself' (DIY) counterculture in which people put ethical and political ideas into practice by using music and other modes of cultural production/expression to highlight both the frustrations and banalities of everyday life, as well as the ideas and institutions that need to be battled if there is any hope of living in a less oppressive world. (p. 10)

Indeed, for Beer (2014, p. 21), the 'discomfort with categorization and definition' is one of the key features of a punk ethos. It is with this sort of view in mind that Kwiatek (2022) suggests that it may be more helpful to think of punk as a family:

> Some bands are punk because the people in them are punks. Some are punk because of the scenes they come from or their fan base. Some bands are punk because of their lyrics or the way their music sounds. Just because there isn't one quality that all and only punk things share doesn't mean there's nothing that it is to be punk. The family resemblance of punk is what allows for the timeless activity of playfully arguing over what is or is not punk. (pp. 7–8)

Like Dunn (2016, p. 9), I think it may be generative to approach punk as an 'open symbol' that is observable through social practices that imagine 'new ways of being' (p. 11). Bestley and colleagues (2019, p. 14) expand on this a little to frame punk as hyperword that encompasses the 'aesthetic, cultural, political and symbolic'.

Accepting the myriad of forms and expressions associated with conceptualizing punk, Bestley (2018, p. 17) points to a common thread as being an oppositional stance, a location from which to challenge and poke fun at the 'parent cultures' it is emergently responsive to. Important here is thinking carefully about the relational aspects of this, as this draws attention to underlying concerns to do with power. In my understanding of punk this is central: the cultural production, expression, and politics of punk offer insight and critique of the structural arrangements and practices that seek to reproduce and expand the domination, discrimination, and control that has been exerted by what Mignolo (2023) describes as the 'colonial matrix of power'.[9] Impacts associated with the colonial matrix of power have reached into all corners of the planet; however, this is experienced and encountered in very different ways within and across cultural and political milieus. The colonial matrix of power can be likened to the 'parental' role in this sense, as it embodies the culture and politics that punk is contextually and temporally responsive to in an ever-growing array of diversity.

Building on this line of thinking there is more to consider, as Bestley (2018, p. 217) expands on, in terms of engaging with punk as something more than an object of study on the one hand, or 'being stereotyped as a colourful subset of progressive political discourse' on the other. Said another way, it would be a mistake or misunderstanding to read this Element and think the suggestion is that educators should simply teach students about punk (an object of study) or to only focus on highlighting the politics of punk (an anarchic and left-leaning discourse). Dines (2015b, p. 130) shares similar lines of concern suggesting that punk can be 'a double-edged sword that both liberates yet also ensnares'. For Dines, while punk can be linked with 'insurrectionary' movements that date back hundreds of years, narrowly conceptualizing punk as an object of academic discourse and/or another expression of political dissent runs the risk of intellectualizing punk in ways that may contravene its 'honour code' and be an 'act of sacrilege' (2015b, p. 132).

This tension can be subsequently exacerbated for those who move into academia or contribute to formal education, which has long been a key institution and technology that is part of the colonial matrix of power machinery. Ultimately, I find much to agree with Dines (2015b, p. 134) when cautioning about the domestication of punk in connection with placing exaggerated emphasis on narrowly defined, or the seemingly more palatable political stances that underpin some expressions of punk. It therefore seems important to hold onto the sorts of ideas shared by Santos and Guerra (2018, p. 222) with regard to the impossibility of freeing oneself from the 'domination and values of inculcation while playing by the rules that dominate and

---

[9] Mignolo (2023) describes coloniality as the 'dark side' of Western modernity in the sense that 'modernity promises salvation, progress, civilization, development and democracy while it conceals coloniality, domination, exploitation, and expropriation' (p. 40). The 'colonial matrix of power', or CMP for short, refers to the mechanisms that reproduce and expand the influences of coloniality.

inculcate'. Hence, there is arguably no middle ground in this respect as educators, if we accept and work with or in the understanding that the learners we engage with deserve an educational experience and process that draws on 'their attributes, diversity and ethos to create a collective, solidary, radical and educational alternative to the individualistic schooling hegemony' (p. 221).

It is the cultural production and politics expressed by punk that offers material, conceptual, political, and social resources that equip people with meaningful 'alternatives [for] the politics of everyday life' (Dunn, 2016, p. 19). The DIY sensibilities of punk open up possibilities for teaching and learning that enable and empower educators and students to engage directly in the politics of knowledge production itself (Santos & Guerra, 2018). For the purposes of this Element, I work from the view that 'punk culture holds the potential to transform educational spaces into sites of empowerment that instil agency and critical thinking skills' (Woods, 2022, n.p.). In other words, punk can be thought of and engaged with by educators as cultural knowledges, artefacts, and languages that can be drawn on for curriculum and pedagogical purposes to question and interrupt the influences of market ideology and human capital paradigms that stem from dominant – parent – cultures.

2.4 Coming Back to Punk

As a teen of the 1980s punk was not something that I actively associated myself with, and in the decades that followed it was simply not something that I thought too much about. This is despite engaging with music, scenes, and ideas connected with punk to varying degrees across the period since then. And this is not to suggest that I actively resisted the label. But that may have been part of the problem; for a long time punk has seemingly been a label that didn't seem to offer much of relevance to me. However, having recently moved back to where I spent my youth and formative years, I had the opportunity to listen and reconnect with current expressions of punk music on the 4ZZZ community radio station out of Meanjin (Brisbane), and as I now approach fifty years of age something has changed. In some ways, this Element is my attempt to retrospectively explore how punk may have influenced my experiences with(in) education throughout my life. It is my hope in doing so that others may find points of connection and interest that open up possibilities for their own educational practices.

How did I arrive at this point? Well, in the months leading up to the early impacts of the Covid-19 pandemic in 2020, before we had the whole of society ordered to stay at home and the university-wide campus shutdowns, I had a particularly early morning tutorial. Rather than run the risk on the motorway of dealing with traffic and being late, I decided every Tuesday that I would go to work prior to the peak hour rush. On the drive I would listen to a radio programme on 4ZZZ called *Concept Warning: Fishing in the Morning*, a punk fishing show (no longer running). At the time bands such as Amyl and the Sniffers, Flangipanis, and the Cosmic Psychos were often played, and along with the tunes there was the banter that offered sociopolitical commentary that was comical, critical, and at times offensive.

On many occasions the commute led to me reflecting on my teens, when I was just out of high school and started going to see live music. This was a time when I was also confronted by the challenges of securing stable work as an unskilled 'youth'.[10] By the late 1980s my adolescence and movement into adulthood was also when I became increasingly politicized. The state of Queensland was still described by many as a police state, the promise of trickle-down economics seemed to be some sort of disingenuous joke, and the world was increasingly saturated by mass-produced material and media empires seemingly designed and run in ways that manipulated the public.[11]

The early 1990s were also a time when I started connecting with people through shared interests that questioned, and in many respects pushed back on, the status quo. Music was an important part of this. Then there were friends (and often friends of friends) that were doing things to bring a sense of community together, such as DIY projects like establishing The Zoo in the Fortitude Valley.[12] The Zoo is likely familiar to many live-music fans with a connection to Meanjin, and it would go on to become an iconic venue and scene which continues to the present. People bringing people together, acting on and in the world, resisting and interrupting what appeared to be a shared understanding and frustration with the absurdity, superficiality, and self-serving interests of the world around us. It was an exciting, interesting, and provocative time.

In the share house where I lived a suburb away from the Valley, friends of mine were enrolled at university and on their way to graduate as teachers. Some went on to have long careers as educators; however, elsewhere (Vass, 2023),

---

[10] With regard to the notion of 'youth', I find much to agree with Lesko (2012) with encouraging educators to critically interrogate the emergence and ongoing influences of this identity label, which was constructed and imposed on young people in problematic ways from the 1950s.

[11] Illustrative of the ongoing reasons why some described it as a police state, there is a paper from Green (2019) discussing events at the 1996 music festival hosted by 4ZZZ. This day was marked by the arrival of significant numbers of police and the shutdown of the event. The festival was held three days after the birth of my first son, and it was the first 'market day' that I had missed in several years. However, as with the research from Green, this event has long lived in the memories of my friends who did attend, and it remains an oft-spoken about historical encounter that serves as a reminder of the dangers and risks of any and all things 'alternative' during those years.

[12] Established in 1992, see www.thezoo.com.au/about for more about the Zoo.

I have written about one friend who became so disenchanted with answers from teacher educators about policies and institutional changes that he walked away from the profession. When looking back on it now, punk sensibilities and ways of living were crucial contributors to my life learning from this period. Punk sensibilities were helping to shape the person that I was becoming, and this subsequently informed my approach to teaching and learning. And, while I haven't always thought about it in these terms, this line of thinking has been further underlined for me during the process of reading and putting this text together. In this sense, my story and experiences have some resonance with others who advocate for punk to be more widely thought about in connection with schooling (see Cordova, 2017; Smith, 2018; Torrez, 2012).

I appreciate that some may view me as not 'punk enough' to be writing a Element with this focus. The sentiments from Furness (2012) in the opening of the edited collection, Punkademics, come to mind here – 'despite being fans of punk music and passionate about the topic – [they] seem to have limited knowledge of punk music and DIY culture, and a level of engagement with punk scenes that is more akin to casual tourism than active participation' (p. 12). While this may be the case up to a point, as Furness (2012, p. 18) goes on to outline, there are many valid reasons why a scholarly interest and approach to punk academic work is warranted, making useful contributions to a range of research fields. In this Element I embrace the sentiments offered in Punkademics to move away from the 'punk-as-style paradigm' that is limited and limiting, and instead shift attention to 'think about what possibilities emerge within and through' punk (Furness, 2012, p. 18). It is in this spirit that I have come to writing the text, and this itself is grounded by the observation that punk invites us to think about and with education policies and practices in ways that have much to offer. Moreover, punk may help make possible discussion of the cultural politics of education and knowledge contestations of schooling in ways that other critical approaches have struggled to make inroads into.

2.5 Getting Skooled in Punk[13]

Even the ABC radio newsreader sounded surprised by what he was reading. 'An unknown band from Brisbane, by the name of the Saints, has earned rave reviews in England for a record it made itself', he intoned. For most Brisbane listeners, it was the first they had heard of the band. (Stafford, 2014, p. 63)

---

[13] The textual styling that drops the 'ch' and instead uses the hard 'k' has already been linked with punk; for example, Dines (2015a) discusses events linked with the travelling community movement in the 1980s that included the Skool Bus, and reference is also made to the Free Skool activities in Canada that were also taking place at this time.

The year was 1976, Meanjin band the Saints had pressed and distributed 500 copies of a single on their own label (Fatal Records), and as hinted at in the quote above the song '(I'm) Stranded' had made its way to England and resulted in being compared to other progenitors of the punk scene. As Stafford (2014) explains, the key members first met in school, like many other bands. Drawn together for more than their shared musical interests, they also shared a disposition and view of the world that questioned and challenged the political, economic, and cultural influences of the period (Stafford, 2014). The Saints seemingly epitomized the sound, attitude, and DIY approach to cultural production that is now synonymous with punk. They attended school in the western suburbs, with the lyrics of '(I'm) Stranded' evoking the angst of growing up in a conservative, constrained, and consumerist world. In doing so, bands such as the Saints struck a chord with some because they spoke of and represented the disenfranchisement and disenchantment that may have resonated with those audiences' own lived experiences. In 1977 the band travelled to London, only to quickly become disillusioned themselves by the limitations and constraints of being associated with punk, and by 1978 the original line-up fell apart (Kaeding, 2007).

Only a couple of years after this, my family moved to the eastern suburbs of Meanjin, and my youth was experienced in the opposite direction to the Ipswich trainline. When we moved to the area there was the remnants of a disused trainline, with the line eventually re-established to enable the hour-long trip into the city, which on weekends only ran every hour and often resulted in lengthy waits at train stations. The intermittent trains didn't run much past midnight, and on occasion waiting to catch the early morning train home contributed to feeling stranded. So too it seemed that little had changed since the time of the Saints more than a decade earlier; the politics were still conservative, the consequences for not socially conforming were stifling, and the promise of economic reforms seemed to largely benefit those who were already privileged.

Reflecting on this period still serves as a reminder for me that many people passing through schooling are offered the promise of economic opportunities, social mobility, and democratic freedom, but part and parcel with education is coming to experience first-hand the institutional arrangements and practices that serve as gatekeepers that control this undertaking. Those who take on a sense of the entrepreneurial 'good citizen' that embraces self-interests to exploit and extract wealth from the planet and other people (Kelly, 2006), may have a chance to live this promise. But for many, they come to see that this is the promise of *cruel optimism* that is like living life ensnared by an impasse, such as an aspiration, that offers access to – but ultimately denies – the societal structures that enable people to get ahead and climb the social, economic, and political ladder (Berlant, 2011, p. 5).

In my experiences as a student and then later a high school educator, it was evident that many young people are well equipped to foster the skills and knowledges that underpin a critical view of the promise offered by trickle-down economics and conservative political decision-making. Indeed, many young people are actively aware and seek connections with others and caring for the planet in ways that challenge the influences of what hooks (2003) describes as *imperialist white-supremacist capitalist patriarchal values*, or what was earlier referred to as the colonial matrix of power (Mignolo, 2023). Moreover, this has long been the case. As outlined by McLaren and Scataburlo-D'Annibale (2004), the groundbreaking work of Willis in the mid-1970s about working-class youth in the UK was a forerunner providing insight into the ways that young people coalesced around shared sociopolitical understandings and practices to establish and maintain cultural milieus that were actively subversive in relation to the dominant culture. Schools were a prominent context in which young people could connect. Writing early in the new millennium, these authors go on to urge for explicit engagement from educators to work with young learners in productive ways to make visible and comprehensible the processes of 'cultural commodification', with a view to then being empowered to interrupt the structural arrangements that maintains the status quo (p. 48).

The critical approach to schooling gestured to here resonates with my own experiences of teaching high school in the wake of the global financial crisis of 2007–8 (aka the GFC). This was the suburban government school introduced earlier, and, as chance would have it, was only a few streets away from my parents' house and the area I had grown up in. There were more than a few students at the school who were children of people that I had attended school with, so I found it easy to relate to many; however, the area had also been gentrifying and private schools had sprung up, which was changing the demographics of the community. Following on from the GFC, many of the students wanted to ask questions about why and how this event happened, the implications from the happenings linked with the GFC, and to better understand the ways it all related to their everyday lived experiences.

Illustrative of this, I can still vividly recall when entering the classroom one day during this period overhearing the chatter between two girls who had gone shopping the previous evening – they were comparing the 'bargains' that they had purchased. In a playfully flippant passing remark, I asked something along the lines about why the shopping spree should be thought of as a bargain, when the true cost to the planet and other people was not adequately accounted for. It was the sort of observation that is easy to imagine will be swiftly ignored by students, but in this instance they asked me to expand on what I was saying. This led to a lesson where we jettisoned what was planned for the day.

Instead, we explored and reflected on the 'cost' in terms of using oil and water, the impacts of pollution, and wages for labour. In essence, it was a story that discussed the processes that enabled cotton grown on one continent to be transported to another continent to be turned into clothing, the potential for environmental damage (in connection with dyes/colouring, transport, oil mining), the sweatshop work to create the clothing, with the apparel then being transported to another continent for sale to people such as themselves. In the end, is buying two t-shirts for $20 a genuine reflection of the 'cost' of producing and then selling these items of clothing? Should being able to purchase shirts, shorts, and jackets that have been produced and sold in this way really be viewed as a 'bargain'? And time didn't allow us to delve too far into considering the role of advertising and marketing for 'youth' audiences.

While I do recall the discomfort and anger that this provoked in some, I can't attest to the long-term impacts of this lesson for the young learners. However, for me it still serves as a powerful reminder of the purposeful and genuine engagement from high school students with actively seeking critical insights about the social, economic, political, and environmental worlds they are stepping into. And more than simply being a 'teachable moment' that was pushed through and linked with learning outcomes or assessment, this was a lesson that fostered a sense of sociopolitical consciousness, being subversive, and caring for community. This was an unplanned lesson, but looking back at it now, I can see that it put punk sensibilities to work in support of teaching and learning by engaging and connecting with the everyday lives of students in meaningful and critically informed ways. In this instance, I also think it was important – or at the least noteworthy – that the lesson didn't entail telling the students what to think, how to act, or that they were to be assessed about particular skills or knowledges from the lesson. The students were able to draw their own conclusions from the knowledge-making practices that stemmed from their own curiosity, questioning, and, at times, shock.

Ultimately, the school years for many have long been understood as a time when questioning and exploring the worlds we inhabit are taken up in earnest. It increasingly becomes personal in the sense that we are restorying our identities as we have experiences and exposure to worlds beyond those of the immediate family. Identity in this usage can be thought of as a sense of self that is fluid, multifaceted, contextual, and dexterous. It is a narrative that we (re)present and (re)negotiate to help locate our self in the social worlds we move through (West-Newman & Sullivan, 2013). The school years are the time when some of us may start rubbing up against the constraints that limit what we can do or where we can go, and often this can be linked with identity markers to do with race, language, gender, sexuality, religion, and able-bodiedness, that are in many cases imposed on us.

With a view to this, the school years – and particularly secondary schooling – have been described by Lesko (2012, p. 94) as a 'panoptical time' for adolescents, due to the teacher gaze of surveillance that has the potential to be internalized by young people in ways that normalize control. Lesko (2012, p. 96), further developing this line of thinking, likens this period to 'the turning point' that positions teachers as the guards to protect the teenage years, exposing 'the underbelly of the colonizers' evolutionary narrative worries over the degeneration and contamination and the anxious scrutiny of physical characteristics, behaviour, and morals for signs of decay'. In returning to the classroom encounter just described, it would have been straightforward and arguably reasonable if I had sanitized the discussion in some form (in essence, to not be overtly political and provocative), as some did seemingly find aspects of the discussion confronting and challenging. And in an era of hyperaccountabilities about the use of time in connection with reporting and assessment, an unplanned lesson such as this may be hard to justify for some. However, to do so would have been to normalize and relegitimate the authority of the colonial matrix of power.

In extending these lines of thinking a little further, we can observe that dominant schooling practices have long struggled to address the sorts of critical questions being asked by some young people about the cultural, economic, and political constructions and impositions of their time and context, and hence the allure of punk. Said another way, schooling has a poor track record with regard to fostering the knowledges and skills that underpin the sort of *critical consciousness* that Freire (2013) spoke of in the 1970s. In the spirit of Freire (1996), learners in the classroom should be thought of as co-investigators who interrogate the limitations and constraints of the social, economic, and political contexts that they inhabit, and in decoding these circumstances and environments they foster the skills, knowledges, and understandings to act on and in the world.

In the absence of schooling contributing to fostering the sort of critical consciousness that enables young people to act on and in the world in the ways they may aspire to, turning to punk offers 'individuals and local communities with resources for self-empowerment and political resistance' (Dunn, 2016, p. 9). As noted in an early contribution from Kahn-Egan (1998, p. 101), punk offers more than tools for interrogation and deconstruction; punk also presents hopeful alternative pathways to subvert dominant ideologies by encouraging students to actively take up political positions. Arguably, the current circumstances are even more dire in the wake of the Covid-19 pandemic, concerns with climate change, ongoing racial and gendered violence, spiralling economic instability, to name a few of the issues contemporary school students encounter. More than ever, schooling needs to find ways to be an act of love and courage, as Freire (2013, p. 34) observed, 'It cannot fear the analysis of reality or, under pain of revealing itself as a farce, avoid creative discussion.' To help with meeting these challenges educators can – and I think should – find ways to draw on punk.

2.6 What about Punk Pedagogies?

The opening of the edited volume from Smith, Dines, and Parkinson (2018, p. 3) states, 'Punk pedagogy lies at the intersection between radical, anarchist and critical pedagogies.' As evident here and observable in the previous subsection, I join many in seeing clear connections between punk and critical approaches to education that are found in the work of Freire, Apple, Giroux, and others (see Santos & Guerra, 2018). These connections are further developed later; for now, it is sufficient to draw attention to this tradition as sharing concerns to do with power, sociopolitical consciousness, and knowledge-making in schooling. These are points of concern that have already popped up across the Element, so does this make punk sensibilities in education another derivation of critical pedagogies?

I would say no: in my way of looking at it, punk pedagogies have the potential to build on and address some of the questions that have been directed towards the perceived limitations of critical pedagogies – such as those outlined by McLaren regarding educators taking up 'leftist' lines of thinking and practice as an 'academic pose or conceit' (as cited in Dines, 2015b, p. 135). But what of the radical and the anarchist? In a similar line of thinking, it is hard to disagree that punk 'breathes new life into analysis of decades-old philosophical, cultural and political thought' (Smith et al., 2018, p. 3). Punk, in this sense, can assist with 'lifting the veil that obscures reality' by establishing pedagogical spaces and practices that directly address the constraints, violence, inequities, and crises that arguably characterizes the current phase of 'modernity' (Santos & Guerra, 2018, p. 222).

For van Dermijnsbrugge (2023, p. 12), punk and anarchy are complementary, with the former emphasizing subversion, resistance, and DIY sensibilities, while the latter encourages non-hierarchical political and social arrangements. In this reading, the synergy between the two is important. Anarchy is typically misunderstood in terms of encouraging the absence of rules or structures, however, it is more helpfully conceptualized in terms of encouraging alternative social and political arrangements to those that are typically vertical. From this, it seems logical – or at least well reasoned – that the punk sensibilities of being subversive, acts of resistance, and adopting DIY approaches may benefit from some form of guiding rules and organization. This seems particularly pertinent for teaching and learning environments which have traditionally been highly stratified and hierarchical; however, schooling would benefit from purposefully moving away from this model.

Despite the promise of critical pedagogies and the encouraging call to be taken up by more educators, in the nearly fifty years these ideas have circulated in educational spaces, there appears to be limited widespread positive impact that can be attributed to this tradition. Indeed, as observed earlier, the influences of neoliberal thinking and practices have been significantly more impactful and corrosive across this span of time. Thus we must consider the caution from Dines (2015b, p. 134) regarding the potential for superficial posturing from academics and educators that can and does denude the politics and real-world impact that critical pedagogies aspire to effect. This is not put forward to tarnish with the same brush all who have taken up critical approaches to teaching and learning – and I would include myself in this critique. But it does seek to recognize that it is easy to say one thing while doing something quite different. It is easy to encourage others to act in ways in which we do not consistently act ourselves. And it is easy to find excuses and explanations for why we don't find ways to support knowledge-making practices that extend beyond the narrow confines of the formal curriculum.

Illustrative of moving beyond being simply derivative of critical pedagogical traditions, the opening section from Stewart and Way's (2023) recent edited collection draws attention to punk pedagogies being further pushed by feminist, antiracist, and decolonizing influences (for example). As they observe, punk pedagogies scholarship has had a tendency to overplay the role of capital (as in being concerned with socioeconomics) and to overlook the significance of coloniality or understanding and engaging with identities from an intersectional perspective. Pushing further in this direction, Bestley, Dines, and Stewart (2023) reflect on scholarly engagements with punk growing significantly across a number of research fields, contributing to interest in and opportunities for interdisciplinarity and synergies to be explored. Illustrative of this, the emergence of the Punk Scholars Network in 2012 is now an international collection of academics that communicate, support each other, and regularly meet to further thinking and practices in support of the punk movement in academia (Bestley et al., 2023). Importantly, these collaborations and musings help push the methodological, theoretical, and reflexive underpinnings of punk scholarship, and by doing so these efforts assist with informing and opening up possibilities for the productive and 'real world' enactment of punk sensibilities, such as in and through pedagogical practices.

Illustrative of work moving in this direction, Romero (2016) outlined a punk-rock pedagogy (PRP) with three pillars that emphasize (1) the significance of context and history, (2) a social justice and explicitly political framework, and (3) the active engagement/involvement with and in community. This is an approach that works in support of decolonizing curriculum and pedagogical practices that has the 'capacity to encourage growth of a divergent knowledge base' (p. 129). Romero (2021) also unpacked the ways that decolonizing punk-rock pedagogies can be educationally transformative by making identity-work more visible and celebrated. More recently, Romero, Estellés, and Grant (2023) explored the generative and curative acts of resistance and solidarity that can arise through the capacity of punk pedagogies to engage deeply and meaningfully with a more-than-human world – a line of thinking expanded on in the next section. A theme across this research from Romero appears to be exploring the ways that punk sensibilities assist with unsettling and purposefully moving away from dominant schooling practices that rely on and reproduce the colonial matrix of power (Mignolo, 2007).

While recent scholarship and research in connection with punk pedagogies draws on and contributes to a broad constellation of theoretical tools which are provocative and valuable for the contemporary sociopolitical environment, there are also the founding sensibilities that warrant further consideration. With a view to this, I would suggest that an additional key facet of how punk sensibilities help with extending beyond the limitations of critical pedagogies is to do with activism and acting on and in the world. While critical pedagogies have always aimed to encourage the enactment of knowledge-making practices within classroom settings, the DIY sensibility is about actively contributing to cultural production, and arguably opens up opportunities for all students to contribute and demonstrate knowledge-making practices.

This is an approach that has a longer tradition in arts-based education, for example music, and I am encouraged here by the contribution from Hess (2019), who builds on critical approaches in the Freirean tradition to outline what she describes as a 'tri-faceted pedagogy' for activist educators by emphasizing 'the importance of building community both locally and in the wider community, honoring and sharing lived experiences for the purposes of expression and resistance, and noticing injustices – not merely the injustices enacted on one's own group, but across identities, in a manner that is intersectional' (p. 156). Gaztambide-Fernández and Rose (2015) share the enthusiastic possibilities revealed by music educators which embrace a *cultural production* approach to teaching and learning as a powerful pedagogical approach to enact social justice practices in the classroom. In their words:

> it allows for living in the present, working with what is, and with who the students are the moment they enter the classroom. It is not an education to learn about the past, or one to prepare for the future . . . it deliberately aims to decentre the norm by focusing on the plural, the contingent, and the unexpected. (p. 469)

Said another way, it is possible to enact knowledge-making practices that express and demonstrate understanding and critical insight through the production of cultural artefacts, and to not rely on students demonstrating their 'learning' with the use of narrowly defined and conceptualized 'academic' texts. I would also suggest that this is an approach that should not be confined to the music- or arts-based classroom, but instead can be learnt from and engaged with more widely in any and all classrooms. Punk sensibilities, in this view, not only encourage us to rethink our pedagogical and curriculum practices; importantly, I would say, a DIY approach to teaching, learning, and assessment in connection with knowledge-making practices offers possibilities for doing skooling in quite fundamentally different and more holistic ways. And for this part of the discussion our attention will turn to composting and the role it can play with helping to decentre – or should I say turn over – the human-centric foundations of schooling.

3 Why Punk Matters for Skooling

3.1 'Animal Rights'[14]

As touched on earlier, it was as a young adult that I started experiencing live music. Many nights out entailed becoming swept up with some sort of punk sensibility. Performances were typically and more immediately a release, not only physically but also in deeper ways. Not that I thought about it this way at the time. This came later, when attending university and encountering ethnomusicology, which opened a doorway to considering the ways music gets in our subconscious, connects us with others, and carries sociopolitical messaging that contributes to (re)producing the worlds we inhabit.

Like others, despite initially associating punk with antiestablishment and nihilistic expressions in response to societal norms, I have come to see that there are communal, curative, and productive ways of conceptualizing punk (Cordova, 2017). Moreover, from the outset punk offered an eclectic, albeit less

---

[14] The album *Animal Rights* (1996) was Moby's fourth studio album. Details about the review were retrieved 10 October 2023 from www.sputnikmusic.com/review/75336/Moby-Animal-Rights/.

identifiable, sense of societal and political hope. For More (2004), punk can be thought of as responding to the 'conditions of postmodernity', an arguably unsurprising response from young people undertaking identity-work in a 'mass-mediated, consumer-driven environment'. Hence, some young people choose to turn-on and up-end the signs and spectacles of dominant culture as a means of 'waging war on society' (More, 2004). And, as already noted, there was a diversity of forms and expressions in which punk took shape; it has always been a socially, politically, and culturally heterogenous movement. Moreover, Dines (2015b, p. 130) offers the reminder that with 'anarcho-punk and queercore, it has also become a place to encapsulate concerns over animal liberation, vegetarianism, women's rights and issues surrounding the LGBT community'.

It is with half an eye on these lines of thinking that this section suggests that one of the limitations of punk scholarship, particularly in connection with education, has been an over-reliance on identity markers that are implicated in the broader reaches of the colonial matrix of power. In other words, punk (sensibilities) and teacher education may both benefit from taking seriously ideas and practices that are emerging with the growing understanding of humans as located within and reliant on the more-than-human world. However, the traces were already in punk activities, as will be explored in the next subsection that looks at the case of vegetarianism or veganism more broadly. Following this, we will delve into what is referred to as post-humanism, though it may be more helpful to engage with this in terms of post-humanist thinking, and in particular attention is directed towards the links between composting and punk. The final subsection returns attention directly towards education to bring the threads together.

By way of finishing this introduction, the subheading ('Animal Rights') is the title of an album from a popular performer at the turn of the millennium, Moby. It was his follow-on album *Play* (1999) that provided an international platform for him, and I do recall his music playing all over the place during this period, though I must confess to never paying much attention to his music or the stories about him. So until recently I had no idea that his music career started in punk bands, or that he has long been a vegan and animal rights campaigner, which goes some way to explaining the title of this album. Having said that, I did find it curious and amusing to encounter a review about the album that opened with this statement: 'I honestly don't know how to start this review other than stating that Moby's *Animal Rights* has just about nothing to do with the fact that Moby is vegan, something that he's arguably become more famous for than his music' (Sugarcubes, 1997). So it is with this in mind that not long ago I received a text from a close friend asking me if I had seen the movie just released by Moby.

3.2 'Really, A Punk Vegan Movie?'

One of my oldest friends, the one that had walked away from using his teaching qualification more than twenty years ago, had just texted me:

'Punk rock was not nihilism; it was principled questioning of everything.' Moby. Good quote that one.

I hadn't heard from him for a while, and in the absence of more context, could do little more than reply with a question mark. He knew that I was working on this Element, so I guessed he was trying to be helpful. But what did a quote from Moby have to do with anything?

It's from his new movie, 'Punk Rock Vegan Movie'. You should watch it. It's free on YouTube.[15]

But this response raised even more questions for me, so I added to my question mark and replied:

Really? Moby, punk, vegan movie?

The phone rang and his boisterous voice playfully chided me for the 'really' part of my reply. I conceded that I may not have been surprised about the punk and vegan part of his message, but Moby, punk, vegan and a movie altogether? In response he burst into laughter:

Oh, is he not punk enough for you Greg!

And I couldn't help but share the laugh.

It was only a couple of years ago that my friend had become a vegan, and catching up now often entailed having some sort of conversation about it all. We had a bit more of a chat, but time didn't allow for a lengthy exchange about the virtues of the movie, and I promised to catch up with it when I had the chance.

A couple of weeks later I found myself with a free afternoon and decided it was a good opportunity to watch the movie. One of the storylines that unfolds is locating veganism within the broader context of punk as it was emerging in the late 1970s and early 1980s in settings such as the UK and US. This includes shedding light on Moby's own involvement with punk bands, which also helps explain the extraordinary collection of people interviewed for the film. As

---

[15] The film was released early in 2023 and can be accessed at www.youtube.com/watch?v=W9q1IidazY8. On the YouTube page with the movie, the following details are shared: 'Punk Rock Vegan Movie is a feature-length documentary written and directed (and shot and scored) by Moby. It looks at the surprising history of punk rock and animal rights activism, features interviews with dozens of punk rock legends, and also cameos from Bagel the dog, the devil, and a boardroom of demons. It's the filmmaker and producers' hope that no one ever pays to see this movie, as it's a labor of love and activism.'

presented in the movie, the questioning and challenging of dominant culture that is shared by punks culminated in what is presented as the logical and seemingly obvious allure of vegetarianism – and from this, veganism. As one of the people interviewed points out, if social conventions and conformity tell you to eat meat (and exploit animals by extension), and you are looking for ways to subvert social conventions and conformity, why wouldn't you become vegan? However, more than simply or superficially being an anticonformist or countercultural expression of independence and agency, the film also explores the underlying ethics and politics that sought to address the exploitation of the environment and animals. Later, this will be discussed in terms of concerns to do with the more-than-human world as an underlying thread permeating some expressions of punk.

However, the film could and should be thought about cautiously. First, the narrative is clearly focused on circumstances within local scenes in the UK and US and doesn't venture beyond this. Hence, it recenters these locations as the primary access points from which to understand or consider punk, and this offers a thin perspective of punk sensibilities. Simply put, the politics of vegetarianism and veganism may not be a sensibility that characterizes punk particularly well as a generalized or universal concern. Adding further to this, it is worth noting that choosing to pursue a vegetarian/vegan lifestyle is far from straightforward – it can be costly, time-consuming, and more challenging in some contexts than others (for example, in accessing the raw materials required to maintain the diet). Moreover, there are skills and knowledges to do with nutrition and maintaining a balanced diet (let alone cooking itself), that also need to be acquired, hence there is an educative dimension.

Illustrative of this, another of the storylines is to do with the shared politics and learnings that were/are often part and parcel of punk scenes. The contribution from early ground-breaking bands such as Crass in the UK were instrumental in this this sense, with later bands learning from recordings and through interactions with band members from Crass. For instance, Captain Sensible from the Damned shares his experiences of staying with Crass in their commune in Epping, learning about and becoming a vegetarian. Similarly, in the US, bands such as Bad Brains – who share that they too were listening to Crass albums – would foreground the further take up of vegetarianism and veganism by punks. And it is within this setting that concerns to do with animal rights, the environment, and health concerns would eventually contribute to the emergence of Straight Edge as a distinct scene within punk.[16] While it is important to keep in mind that punk is diverse, as is noted in the film, there has also long been

---

[16] The film explains that Straight Edge emerged in the early 1980s with a focus on rejecting 'alcohol + drugs and mindless hedonism', and by the mid 1980s this had expanded to embrace vegetarianism and later veganism.

a communal element, which is highlighted with the passage in the film that explores the challenges of trying to be a vegetarian or vegan while on the road and touring in the 1980s and 1990s. Evidently this was far from easy, and learning from and with each other was necessary for practical reasons, in addition to the political and philosophical lessons that went hand in hand with this.

In the end, it is hard to disagree with the central premise and theme that is returned to repeatedly across the film. Punk was, and is, about questioning and challenging the status quo. The quiet acceptance and acquiescence of the broader community with regard to the ongoing commercial exploitation and industrial-scale cruelty towards animals and the environment is exactly the sort of status quo that warrants disruption and intervention. It is hardly surprising that punk activities have culminated in the production and sharing of knowledges and resources that include a strong emphasis in this direction. So, to further consider these lines of thinking, we are going to start thinking about the more-than-human world. This gestures to efforts to decentre the privileging and prioritizing of humans, an interruption that aims to rupture the hubris that has conceptualized everything in the world as available to be exploited and manipulated to serve the interests of humans. To bridge into the next section, I share lyrics from one of the more vocal and visible punk contributors to these efforts. They come from Earth Crisis and their song 'New Ethic' (1995):[17]

This is the new ethic.
Animals' lives are their own and must be given respect.
Reject the anthropocentric falsehood that maintains the oppressive hierarchy of mankind over the animals.
It is time to set them free.
Their lives reduced to biomachines in the factory, farm and laboratory.
Dairy, eggs and meat, fur, suede, wool, leather are the end products of torture, confinement and murder.
I abjure their use out of reverence for all innocent life.
Wildlifes' right to live in peace in their natural environment without this civilization's interference can no longer be denied.
Must no longer be denied.
To make a civilization worthy of the word civilized, the cruelty must end, starting within our own lives.

---

[17] From the album *Destroy the Machines*, written by Karl Buechner. Lyrics retrieved 18 February 2023 from https://genius.com/Earth-crisis-new-ethic-lyrics.

3.3 Punk Composting, (Post)coloniality and the Time to Make Kin Not Babies

Recently, I read a paper from Bell and Ream (2021) in which they talk about the importance of reimagining how teachers and learners engage with the stories of the colonial era. Coloniality is not to be thought of as a 'unilinear chronology of events' (Mignolo, 2007); rather, colonialism continues into the present, and hence colonization is better thought of as a process (Wolfe, 2016). More to the point, attention needs to move beyond addressing the *content* of global inequalities as they are evident within economics, politics, race, gender, and so on (Mignolo, 2023). Instead, we must interrogate and address the *terms* – the 'assumptions, beliefs, taken for granted' – that established and maintain the status quo with regard to global inequalities and discrimination (p. 45). This gestures to changes in one's sense of self, and relationship to and with the worlds we move through. This calls for changes to the identity-work that students – and by extension I would suggest teachers also – undertake in connection with their school years.

Bell and Ream (2021) describe an approach for reconceptualizing teaching and learning as being like composting, and they liken teachers and learners to being 'Compostists [that] are from the soil, work the soil, and live within soiled worlds.' In this usage, composting gestures to processes of change and identity-work that are grounded in places and the peoples we encounter. Imagine this happening across our school years as the seasons come ago, with layers of 'learnings' settling on and within our sense of self. It is a constant and ongoing process, with the 'old' and the 'new' coming together, and then again, again . . . and again. Hence, composting is cyclical, with death and decay feeding just as swiftly into nutrition and growth. In support of this process, composting benefits from being turned over, cared for, and fed. So, rather than images and metaphors of teachers caring for students as seeds or saplings that grow out of and live a life above the earth, perhaps the notion of composting may be useful for opening up different and more fertile lines of thinking.

In connection with skooling, these lines of thought invite thinking about the learner and teacher in ways that differ from dominant discourses about these subject positions. For instance, here I am mindful of observations such as Gobby and Millei (2022, p. 51), about teacher education continuing to provoke and invoke a sense of educators as 'entrusted with the authority to fill the minds of children (with "school knowledge") and secure their natural and moral development'. This offers a familiar view of students as passive recipients of an education that is done to and on them by those in positions of power. This is a model and set of relations in schooling that we need to move away from.

And I find much to agree with Bell and Ream's (2021, p. 108) suggestions regarding compostism because it 'speaks to the nonlinear and asymmetrical relationality that exists' between place and people; between teachers, students, classrooms, and the world beyond the school gate. In settler societies such as Australia, this opens up opportunities to reconsider the foundations of, and the entanglements between and within, colonialism, race, gender, class, the more-than-human-world, and so much more.

These topics are challenging to engage with in depth, detail, and the sort of nuance required in teacher education programmes, especially when considering the current neoliberal influences in higher education. In the context of Australia, studies are fragmented into courses (or subjects) that are typically twelve or thirteen weeks long, and emphasis is narrowly (and increasingly) placed on professional standards. Similar lines of concern can be raised for six- or eight-week sequences of learning developed and delivered during the primary or secondary years of schooling. One of the challenges with compressed time-frames, which are concurrently ensnared by standardized curriculum and learning outcomes, is that it lends itself to relatively brief or superficial nods to the violence of colonialism that has shaped and continues to influence the worlds that we all inhabit.

There may be many reasons why teaching and learning about contested and complex issues such as colonialism, race, gender, and so on evoke waves of resistance, surprise, guilt, anger, disbelief, and uncertainty, all of which require the kind of time and care for exploration that is seemingly difficult to find. My efforts in secondary and tertiary education have framed it in terms of requiring critical reflection, ongoing learning, and taking responsibility for future steps, not for the actions of those in the past. And that it is better to genuinely attempt to engage with complex and contentious knowledges in teaching and learning, and to learn from this undertaking, than to not attempt anything in the first place. This seems to suffice on occasion; however, it also often leaves me with a sense of not quite hitting the mark.

As with Bell and Ream (2021), I agree that teaching and learning must be more than a process of recognizing the violence of the past and its ongoing implications. Instead, it is about 're/con/figuring' who we are, with a view to then taking 'response-ability' for our actions going forward.[18] Educators will play a key role if this is to occur, or as Haraway (2016, p. 100) encourages, it

---

[18] The hyphens and forward slashes in these texts are an invitation to slow down reading and thinking. For example, use of words such as reconfiguring or responsibility are familiar and easily wash over the reader. However, hyphenating 'response-ability' is not as familiar and easily passed over, and rather than being one word (albeit a complex one with many meanings), the reader is reminded that there are two words – response and ability – that warrant further attention.

will require those with 'intense commitment and collaborative' playfulness to reimagine and enact practices in ways that accept the earth is full of refugees, without refuge. Haraway (2015) argues that there has been a 'game changing shift'; it is no longer political, economic, technological, or social changes of scale, speed, or complexity that impact on the world, but more fundamentally 'changes in kind'. Hence, those of us involved in education urgently need to draw on teaching and learning resources that are better equipped to critically interrogate the cultural practices that have dominated the colonial epoch. In an effort to shift not only our thinking, but the very ways we talk about things, Haraway (2016) uses a different term to describe the current moment: the *Chthulucene*.[19]

In the hope for reinstating some form of 'multispecies ecojustice', Haraway (2016, p. 161) puts forward the suggestion that it is time to 'make kin not babies'. This too is a move away from the trappings of dominant languaging practices. Kin-making gestures towards notions of identity-work that are expansive; it is a relational and locational turn of phrase to help restory the more-than-human worlds that all species inhabit and rely on. Hence, the reminder that we 'are all compost', sharing worlds that are seemingly on the eve of collapse, and with that, extinction. This also accepts that we are all composting, already in the process of being transmogrified, and therefore we should be far more attentive to the conditions, why this is the case, and the potential effects from this (Hamilton & Neimanis, 2018, p. 503).

As an entree point for this, storytelling comes into view, as 'stories emerge from specific histories, and they engender material effects' (Hamilton & Neimanis, 2018, p. 515). It is an explicitly feminist telling of tales that invokes 'particular kinds of relationships between humans with the more-than-human world' (p. 516). And, importantly, it is not as though anything and everything should go into the compost pile and the stories we tell. Rather, careful attention must be extended to consider whose, or what, interests are served or undermined by our efforts.

In a recent special issue, Nxumalo, Nayak, and Tuck (2022) call for recentring the entanglements of nature–culture relations in and through schooling. They encourage the enactment of 'pedagogies grounded in radical relationality that takes seriously the knowledge-making capabilities of the more-than-human world' (p. 98). Composting is well worth considering in this regard, and as

---

[19] Haraway (2016, p. 2) defines this term: '*Chthulucene* is a simple word. It is a compound of two Greek roots (*khthôn* and *kainos*) that together name a kind of timeplace for learning to stay with the trouble of living and dying in response-ability on a damaged earth.' And, as she has noted elsewhere, 'These real and possible timespaces are not named after SF writer HP. Lovecraft's misogynist racial-nightmare monster Cthulhu (note spelling difference)' (Haraway, 2015, p. 16).

Neimanis and McLachlan make the case, composting can be conceptually useful as an approach for engaging in the classroom with existing resources and insights that can be turned over and mulched together to 'nourish new possibilities' and ways of 'co-worlding new and latent possibilities (p. 219). Central to composting are efforts to explicitly value and deliberately repurpose 'extant matters' in support of worlding in different ways (Hamilton & Neimanis, 2018, p. 505). Does this now point to a way of returning to punk more explicitly? Punk is a movement and ethos that is underpinned by efforts that work towards turning over the excesses of modernity with a view to worlding in different ways.

3.4 Punk and Composting for Skooling

Norton (2018) identifies the 1970s band Crass as pointing in this direction. From the outset Crass were drawing attention to sociopolitical concerns that extended to the environment. While this may be viewed in a humanist tradition in terms of saving the environment for the enjoyment of people, the views put forward in 'Punk Rock Vegan Movie' (discussed earlier) suggest that concerns to do with the relationship between people and the more-than-human world were always present for some punk contributors.

By the 1990s the compost of earlier punks was being turned over, and the mulching encouraged more explicit and radical eco-justice calls in response to the growing evidence about the impact people were having on the planet. As Norton (2017) shares, the increasing diversity of punk when coupled with broader sociopolitical shifts gave rise to bands such as Oi Polloi and clearly articulated concerns about the more-than-human world. In the US a collection of bands such as Earth Crisis, Youth of Today, Gorilla Biscuits, and others linked with Straight Edge were addressing similar lines of thinking, while scenes were also evident all around the world. Emphasizing this point, a compilation box set released in 2000 entitled *More Than the X on Our Hands: A Worldwide Straight Edge Compilation*, includes bands from forty-one countries (Haenfler, 2006, p. 10). However, the research from Haenfler (2006, p. 65) about the Straight Edge movement also offers the reminder that these bands were not anomalies with regard to espousing 'the virtues of clean life; resisting mainstream society; supporting one's friends; staying positive; and a variety of social issues including racism, sexism, and the environment'.

Sharing lines of thinking with the compostists and punks that have been drawn on for these ruminations, Snaza and Weaver (2014) remind us that education is increasingly implicated in the sort of post-humanist turn gestured to. Indeed, there are growing numbers of those involved in education that recognize and seek remedies to the role and contribution of schooling with reproducing 'the human'. For example, these concerns framed a special issue on critical post-human thinking, with guest editors Nxumalo and Vintimilla (2020) outlining the possibilities that open up by drawing on this approach to help with reconceptualizing how we understand, work with, and represent learner subjectivities in schooling. As encouraged across the special issue, there remains much to be explored and acted on to better establish 'what it might look like to unsettle anthropocentrism while also attending to its colonial and racist underpinnings, which continue to construct racially marginalized children and families as less-than-human' (Nxumalo & Vintimilla, 2020, p. 272).

Pointing in this sort of direction, Mayes and colleagues (2019, p. 2) invite the reader to 'rethink the concept of educational inequalities beyond human relations' in the deindustrializing city of Geelong, Australia. Their discussion about affect, spatiality, and materiality provokes the reader to question the humanist foundations that intertwine and reproduce inequality and schooling discourses, culminating in pathways of possibilities for 're-imagining more equitable relations in conditions of human and climatological precarity' (Mayes et al., 2019, p. 10). Beyond this, other contributors such as Taylor (2020) and Lindgren (2020) are also illustrative of encouraging critical thinking about the importance of actively linking identity-work during the school years with fostering more-than-human understandings. With a view to these lines of thinking, we can see that it is a very particular type of human subject that worryingly sits at the apex of the hierarchy of the modernity project and maintains this power through ongoing exploitation, extraction, and controlling the means of violence. Doesn't this, then, invite questions about what education might look, sound, and feel like if we purposefully seek ways to decentre the reproduction of 'the human'?

Many of the educators that I work with are well aware of the challenges ahead of them. They are tasked with managing behaviour, improving literacy and numeracy, fostering future leaders (in discipline or subject-specific fields), ushering young people into the workforce, and so much more. They are also informed about statistics to do with closing achievement gaps, exclusions, attendance, post-school transitions, medical conditions, and more. Then they are challenged to consider the social, economic, political, and historical traces that could or should help them develop an understanding of the life worlds of the students and communities they connect with. And there are also the challenging sociopolitical questions that respond to world-shaping events. At the time of writing, this includes the recent unsuccessful referendum in Australia about the Voice to parliament, war in Ukraine and Gaza, and the climate change conference (COP 28) agreement (which seemingly didn't involve some countries most impacted by climate change). Then there are ongoing conversations about the Black Lives Matter movement, domestic violence, growing economic inequities ... the list goes on. There is much to learn. But perhaps there is even more to unlearn.

Offering a further reminder of the political context of schooling, within Australia we recently had conservative voices that sought to silence or contain the scope, scale, and content of the curriculum as enabling critical conversations. For example, in 2021 during a heated debate regarding the review of the national curriculum, a motion was put forward to the Federal government to ensure that influences from critical race theory would have no presence in the revised curriculum.[20] However, this is arguably a relatively minor illustration of this when compared with settings such as the US, as Chapman and Hobbel (2022) recently discussed, with many states legislating laws that can identify and penalize individual teachers for teaching concepts to do with race, sex, meritocracy, White privilege, and more. This serves as a reminder that even if willing, able, and committed, for some teachers there are constraints imposed on them that mean it is personally and professionally risky to ask questions and push back on current education policy arrangements. Thus, it is arguably no surprise that many of those who make it through and into the teaching profession also make their way out again within five years of embarking on this career (Heffernan, et al., 2019).

On more than a few occasions I have had encounters with (future) educators where they have called it all a pile of garbage – the curriculum and pedagogical tools they are encouraged to engage with are not fit for purpose. The education policies that create the structural arrangements are some distance from the lived day-to-day reality of being in schools. The education lecturers and researchers they encounter are full of big words and theories that seem to have no relevance for schooling. And on more than a few occasions it has been hard to disagree. However, it is not my intention to fret in pessimistic ways! Just as the compostists have encouraged us to rethink our efforts in view of the possibilities for nourishing growth and vitality that open up with the more-than-human turn, and the punks who took, turned over, and returned the signs, symbols, and excesses of modernity to foster sensibilities about caring for communities, sociopolitical consciousness, and being DIY, there are many reasons to be positive. I am firmly of the view that schooling can be so much more for many students than is currently the case. And the next section will turn attention in this direction, to consider the possibilities that open up for teachers and students by working with punk in the classroom.

---

[20] For more on this you could read the article in the Conversation, https://theconversation.com/the-senate-has-voted-to-reject-critical-race-theory-from-the-national-curriculum-what-is-it-and-why-does-it-matter-163102, accessed 20 October 2023).

4 Working with Punk in the Classroom

4.1 'I'm Like All the Pop Stars on Commercial Radio'[21]

Attention will return to directly consider the context of teaching and learning in the classroom. However, to foreground this, it might be helpful to give some attention to what could be thought of as another punk sensibility, related to tensions between ideas about authenticity, and the criticism thrown around in connection with the perception of 'selling out'. The commodification and marketing of 'punk' has cast a long shadow, arguably starting off and often typified by the efforts of Malcom McLaren, Vivian Westwood, and others in the UK from the mid-1970s, creating and profiting from the crafting of representations that symbolized a form of punk (Bestley & Ogg, 2022, p. 36). The worldwide popularity of Green Day in the 1990s also offers an illustration of how this plays out. In this case, despite the band's foundations within a local scene their latter commercial success raised questions about their integrity and punk credentials (Dale, 2016, p. 35). While it is not my intention to venture too far down this path, there is no avoiding the point that visual and aural aesthetics of punk are part and parcel of the politics of scenes, and with this come voices that seek to establish and maintain notions of being insiders or outsiders.

Dale (2016) playfully picks up on this line of thinking to invite deeper consideration about the loosely thrown around refrain about anybody being able to play and contribute to the cultural production of punk. As he explains, the notion of amateurism as being a hallmark of punk has led to the curious situation where the musical skills of some performers have been deliberately toned down, while also championing DIY practices in ways that seemingly impose constraints on the economic viability and stability of those contributing to the cultural production of punk. The tension between some sort of amateurism in comparison with the trappings of professionalism does indeed appear to be a vexed issue, albeit one that likely consumes no shortage of banter between and within punk scenes. I am tempted to draw further on Dale's (2016) words here: 'The aspiration that punk should entirely divorce from the mainstream economy is always an already failed project' (p. 35). He suggests, for eminently pragmatic reasons, that 'uncomfortable compromises' may be more common than is widely assumed.

At stake are questions and concerns to do with how cultural resources are produced and shared with others – such as who has creative and intellectual control of any given project, who profits or benefits from the sharing of the

---

[21] From the song 'I'll 'Ave ya', on the album *Hot Dogma* (1990) from the band TISM (or This is Serious Mum), lyrics retrieved 30 October 2023 from https://genius.com/Tism-ill-ave-ya-lyrics.

resources, and so on. In part, this returns to threads of earlier discussion regarding the sociopolitical circumstances that punk is associated as emerging within and is responsive to, and the broader influences of neoliberal thinking. In essence, is there a tipping point when balancing the politics and integrity within any given punk scene, with accepting financial support from the commercial sector or public funding? Here we can gesture to the rise of what have been described as the 'cultural industries', or more recently the 'creative industries' (Hesmondhalgh, 2008; Lee, 2017; Newsinger, 2015). The latter is particularly pertinent to the ideas central to this Element, and this is because of the influences of the dominant policy environment in which 'creativity' has been co-opted in ways that endorse and further inequities and exploitation (Hesmondhalgh, 2008, p. 567).

In essence, there is much to agree with when worrying about the role and influence of the creative industries as resulting in cultural production increasingly operating in support of companies and profit, and decreasingly as a form of expression from and for the interests of society more broadly (Newsinger, 2015). It is perhaps with this line of thinking in mind that Dunn (2012) advocates the import of maintaining a DIY sensibility and approach to cultural production. As he explains, while big business can and does 'appropriate and assimilate' ideas, politics, and representations, these tend to remain a vapid and insipid simulacrum of punk (p. 234). Nonetheless, we should remain wary of romanticizing notions of DIY sensibilities as means of insulating some sort of authentic sense of what is or isn't punk. It is a false binary to imagine this in oppositional terms – that there are 'true' or pure forms of punk, in comparison with 'commodified' or corrupted forms (Jones, 2021, p. 63). Instead, making efforts to hold onto what Dines (2015b, p. 132) describes as the 'precarious balance' regarding form and content is important to being aligned with a 'genuine' punk sensibility.

The role of the state, big business, and the commodification of culture has of course long been a hallmark of what punk scenes have been responding (subversively) to. However, as Dale (2016) hints, to suggest that resonating with punk sensibilities should necessitate forgoing security, stability, and quality of life may not appeal quite so widely. It is a tension that emerges in punk cultural artefacts, such as the lyrics used as the subheading for this section, which come from the band TISM. At a little over two minutes in length the bulk of the song repeats the refrain 'you look like' followed by a collection of names from politics, history, and pop culture. I had to look up a couple of these myself; I must have missed Magilla Gorilla entirely in my youth, and I was equally unfamiliar with who George Shultz was. The song culminates in the lament that the band is being played on a prominent commercial radio station, 'like all the other pop stars'.

For some, TISM are perhaps more pop than punk. Debating this is not likely to be helpful at this stage. For me, the politics, irreverence, and their challenge to think critically about dominant culture that is a consistent theme of TISM across the years are illustrative of punk sensibilities at work. As will be explored in the next subsection there are many ways to be, express, and resonate with punk sensibilities. Following on from this, attention turns to using a recognizable and popular film to explore ideas about what punk sensibilities could look like when adopted as a whole-of-class approach to teaching and learning. Next, the focus turns to look at how and why drawing on punk sensibilities in the classroom has links with well-established pedagogical and curricular practices that draw on the cultural assets that students are familiar with. Lastly, the threads are drawn together to explore how and why punk sensibilities in skooling can foster the sort of sociopolitical consciousness that opens up pathways for young learners to act on and in the world as agents of change.

4.2 Not That Sort of Punk

At a gig I attended recently, the aesthetics that are often associated with punk were clearly on display – some people were dressed in ways that conveyed this sense through hair styles and clothing (yes, there were people with spiked mohawks), aspects of the performances lyrically and musically conveyed it (some of the songs were short, loud, a bit angry, and explicitly political), and the venue itself had all the hallmarks of a DIY project (it looked like a reclaimed shed in an industrial area near a train station). As I was sitting there, the thought occurred to me that if looking, sounding, attending places, and behaving in certain ways are supposed to be or mean something is particularly punk – that there are codified rules to follow and boundaries to maintain – then what sort of punk might I be?

However, this representation doesn't tell the whole story of what was going on. It was late in the afternoon, I was wearing a flora-and-fauna-inspired shirt (and many others were dressed in equally unremarkable ways), the collection of performers were soloists on semi-acoustic guitars (other than a harmonica joining in on a few songs) that included ballads in their repertoire, people politely queued for their drinks and to order food, and there was a welcoming and warm environment for all to share and participate in. There was a lot that could be described as not typically associated with punk.

As I continued to ponder this scene, I was drawn to the idea that if punk is to mean anything for me, it is about people from any and all walks of life coming to appreciate and understand that the creative industries were taken over by big business with the support of the political elite, and there are fundamental problems over the last few decades for individuals, groups, and the more-than-human world that stem from this project (Jones, 2021; Lee, 2017; Newsinger, 2015). To be sure, the foundations of this situation precede the mid-twentieth century; however, as observed by Lesko (2012, p. 117–118), the rise of postwar mass production, when coupled with notions of democratic freedoms and opportunism that are entwined with capitalism, has established and promoted waves of social and political practices where the worth and contribution of individuals and groups are largely equated with the capacity to purchase and consume goods or services. Sandlin and McLaren (2010) describe it as consumerist behaviour becoming a cognitive and moral organizer of life that both encourages and requires the ongoing reworking of our identities – albeit with the caveat that this is largely within capitalist, industrialized, and wealthy contexts.

These massive creative industries are hence in the business of producing and reproducing certain types of people – those who support, invest their lives in this system, and seek to protect it. Education is also heavily implicated, if not actively integrated, in these industries. Indeed, according to Spring (2010), the foundations of this can be observed late in the nineteenth century in contexts such as the US, with education policies, curriculum, and pedagogies across the twentieth century being designed with the explicit purpose of teaching learners to become good consumers in their post-school years. So when I think about being punk, it is associated with people seeing this system for what it is, calling it out, and seeking to go about undermining or challenging it in innovative and provocative ways. And this is what I observed – or at least think I did – while sharing drinks with friends on that warm Saturday afternoon in Meanjin.

In view of these ideas, I associate punk with actively thinking of the self as part of and contributing to disrupting the status quo. Which is of course easier said than done. Perhaps, as Dines (2015b, p. 132) suggests, this is particularly so in the context of formal education, where the notion of punk itself as being linked with pedagogy may be viewed as an anathema. In this vein, he reflects on the effects of formal schooling being increasingly marketed as a competitive service industry, with educators packaging up palatable and attractive goods for student consumers (p. 134). As outlined earlier, the impacts associated with neoliberal thinking and practices across the education sector have already significantly altered the experiences, opportunities, and possibilities for teachers and learners. There is significant pressure to *graciously submit*, while the risks for gracious subversion likely seem beyond reach for some. For example, if we think of the core touchstones of curriculum, pedagogy, and assessment, how much scope for being creative, unconventional, or even radical, is genuinely available to a great many educators?

Illustrative of how this can play out, albeit in a relatively minor way, both as a high school teacher and now increasingly in teacher education, it is unsettling and at times confusing when students push back on teaching, learning, and assessment practices that are designed to give them scope to be knowledge producers. In such instances, the encouragement that there is more than one way to approach assessment, or that a task requires demonstrating independent thinking rather than producing the 'correct' response, can at times elicit strong reactions of resistance and resentment. During teaching and learning itself, but also increasingly on the end of semester evaluations, students can be vocal – and at times quite personal – with their responses. For some educators, the risks associated with trying to be creative or unconventional may be too great. This fosters conditions in which becoming the 'domesticated radical' emerges, with the emphasis on critical pedagogy sidelined in problematic ways, rather than 'facilitating space in which learning might occur, knowledge might be generated and, ultimately, oppression might be resisted' (Dines, 2015b, p. 135). The liminality and uncertainty of teaching and learning must be embraced and accepted, or we run the risk of 'selling-out' as the teacher using punk as a gimmick.

As already observed, one of the central concerns underpinning this Element is the identity-work of learners. If I had a couple of dollars for every time I heard (or shared) an utterance about the value of relationships and knowing/understanding students, I suspect that I would have stopped working long ago. However, despite the visibility of this focus in education, it is also hard not to see and hear that this remains one of the most vexing and time-consuming concerns for many (Egeberg, McConney & Price, 2021). Indeed, rather than placing greater emphasis on behaviour management strategies, as remains familiar or desirable to many, a study from Egeberg and colleagues (2021, p. 121) highlights that greater attention should be directed towards classroom management practices that include 'caring relationships, high expectations and opportunities for engagement, participation and contribution'. For many students, not being heard, understood, feeling valued, or liked by educators remains a key worry linked with disengagement (Martin & Collie, 2019); whereas a greater number and quality of positive student–teacher relationships significantly expands the 'academic repertoire' of learners, and from this leads to improved personal, interpersonal, and academic schooling experiences (Martin & Collie, 2019). Clearly, something needs to change about how we understand, work with, and reimagine our approaches for supporting identity-work in the classroom.

4.3 'One Great Show Can Change the World'

It is not uncommon for punk to draw on and in some form invert resources made by the creative industries, for the purpose of subversive critique. In this section, I am going to try and walk a fine line in this direction by engaging with a Hollywood story depicting a class of students and teacher as they learnt from and with each other in ways that disrupt the representation of a traditional classroom. The film is *School of Rock* (Linklater, 2003), and it is worth noting up front that I maintain concerns regarding the stereotypically problematic representations of people portrayed – the troublesome and antisocial drummer; the high-achieving class prefect; the costume designer; and even the elitist and high socioeconomic parents to name a few. Said another way, the film relies on lazy tropes as the basis for what is supposed to be humorous, seemingly missing the point that these could be offensive and actively unhelpful. And, most concerningly, the lead protagonist depicts (and ultimately celebrates) the deceptions, recklessness, selfishness, and potentially dangerous actions of somebody pretending to be a teacher. However, despite my reservations, I also think that it draws attention to the merits of pedagogically getting to know, value, and work with the strengths and cultural resources that students arrive at the school gate with. Hence, this film is worth giving some attention to.

School of Rock (Linklater, 2003), for those of you who are not familiar with it, portrays the efforts of Dewey Finn (played by Jack Black) to impersonate his flatmate and former bandmate as the classroom teacher in an elite private primary school.[22] The backdrop to the story includes Finn's failed attempts to become a rock star, his efforts to seek revenge for being kicked out of a band, and the urgency to secure money to pay his rent. Once arriving to take over the temporary teacher role, a picture of his disinterest with regard to the students or teaching is offered. Sleep is high up on his list of things to do, as is waiting for the end of the school day so Finn can resume attempts to recruit new bandmates. The catalyst for change occurs when the students attend their music lesson and he overhears the virtuoso efforts of students in the class.

The story subsequently unfolds in typical Hollywood feelgood ways. Finn encourages the virtuosos to play rock music in a band, roles are subsequently found for all the class members, including the band manager, costume designer, sound and lighting engineer, and even those with security responsibilities to help ensure the school principal does not discover what is going on. Ultimately, his plan is to take the class on an 'excursion' to play in an upcoming battle of the bands, with himself as a performer. Despite the plan being foiled thanks to his housemate's partner discovering Finn's impersonation, the students take it upon themselves to organize the bus driver, pick up Finn on the way to the competition, and put on what he had earlier described as the 'one great show that can change the world'. The parents rush to the venue, only to be overwhelmed and

---

[22] For more about the film, see https://schoolofrock.fandom.com/wiki/School_of_Rock.

impressed by the performances of the students. All ends well. Hopefully, that is sufficient to give you a broad sketch of the film.

So, you may be asking yourself, why talk about this film in the context of this Element? To consider this, I want to return attention to punk sensibilities that leverage off the ideas from Way (2021) to show how and why they may be broad enough in scope that they assist with provoking thinking about some of the practices portrayed in *School of Rock*. The first of these is to do with the value of establishing and caring for community; second, there is the role of being subversive in productive and generative ways; next, the import of fostering sociopolitical consciousness to empower people to act on and in the world; and lastly there is taking on the commitment to support a DIY approach to getting things done. In accepting these punk sensibilities as being broad enough to stretch across different contexts, when working with them we should remain mindful that punk should not become static or bounded by any particular set of rules.

When drawing on these punk sensibilities to consider *School of Rock* (Linklater, 2003), establishing a sense of community within the classroom is central to what Finn works towards once his attention moves to actively engaging with the class. Finn is shown getting to know and understand the talents and dispositions of the learners; concomitant with this is developing an understanding of the life-worlds of individuals beyond the classroom, and he conveys an interest and commitment to the holistic well-being of students. Next, on some levels, the entire premise of the project to take the class to the battle of the bands encourages a subversive approach to schooling – humour derives from the point that most schools would likely never support this sort of activity; indeed the competition organizers would likely be equally unsupportive.

The weekly timetable is quickly discarded, with familiar classroom activities upended to prioritize often student-led activities in support of the whole-of-class project. And there are also scenes where Finn encourages the students to understand and resist the control and influence of 'the man', which represents bureaucratic, political, and corporate control. In another scene, he assigns specific bands/albums to expand the musical horizons of students beyond the confines of the classical genre. These instances are again illustrative of a whole-of-student approach, where the constraints and limitations of the formal curriculum and assessment are resisted, but learning remains central to the activities.

With regard to fostering sociopolitical consciousness, while perhaps not as overtly evident in some respects (remember, it is still a mainstream Hollywood blockbuster), there are instances where Finn encourages learners to have autonomy and agency with their contribution to the class-based project, for example, the costume and lighting design students, while others are invited write and perform their own songs. Indeed, the theme song for the film, which is performed by the class at the battle of the bands, could itself be viewed as representing a form of sociopolitical consciousness ... are you singing along to this yet ... *'Baby we was making straight A's, but we were stuck in a dumb daze. Don't take much to memorize your lies, I feel like I've been hypnotized ...'*[23].

Lastly, there is the DIY approach, which is key to the meaningful involvement of so many learners in the whole-of-class project. Examples of this include those on the security detail setting up cameras and making videos to deceive the principal, and the classroom prefect's deception with the school bus driver who unwittingly takes the class on the excursion. In these and other cases, the representation in the film implies that the students (already) have the skills and independence to demonstrate initiative and to problem-solve through actively undertaking the tasks at hand – rather than having things done for them.

To be sure, the film needs to be engaged with critically and not accepted at face value in educational terms. Teaching and learning in the 'real world' is never as neat and tidy. Individual teachers are unable to go off on this sort of project-based learning trajectory and disregard the formal curriculum. And, as noted earlier, there are a number of problematic stereotypes. Moreover, and to reiterate the point, in no way is it being suggested that non-accredited or committed professionals should take responsibility for teaching in educational settings. Having offered these caveats, I would invite you to also consider how and why some of the punk sensibilities depicted in the film could be enacted and assist with classroom practices more widely.

To begin with, there are good reasons for finding time and different ways to meaningfully and holistically understand the learners in our classrooms and to foster a (punk-inspired) sense of community. This supports working with learners to find and pursue their own life pathways, rather relying on assumptions or ideas (that stem largely from the adult world) about what may or may not be 'best' for learners. Finding this time may require being subversive with what is being prioritized, and it is okay to do so because there are pedagogical reasons why this is justifiable. Moreover, some rules and regulations are genuinely divisive, unfair, and discriminatory. There are well-founded reasons why students can and should be encouraged and empowered to call these out for what they are.

Across my time in education, I cannot recall meeting someone who did not articulate the desire to work with learners with a view to developing the skills, knowledges, and capacity to act on and in the world – to actively foster sociopolitical consciousness in some form. But the busy-ness of schooling

---

[23] See full lyrics at https://genius.com/School-of-rock-school-of-rock-lyrics.

often deflects attention from these efforts. And meaningfully fostering sociopolitical consciousness and the ability to act on and in the world are perhaps more needed than ever, given that future generations are inheriting a litany of social, economic, political, and environmental concerns that demand their attention. Likewise, the notion of thinking global, but acting on and in the local, is achievable for any and all learners in schooling. In other words, a DIY approach entails drawing on resources or materials that are available, and hence it doesn't require or need to wait for trickle-down support to arrive.

4.4 Punk Lessons from Asset-Based Approaches Like Hip Hop Pedagogies

The lines of thinking developed across this section suggest that punk sensibilities can contribute to classrooms being locations where learners are enabled to become critically aware about their own positionality, dominant culture, institutional arrangements, and from this, to become active agents of change 'constructing new realities of their own design' (Kahn-Egan,1998, p. 100). Culture (and language) come back into view here, and it is worth the reminder that culture is a foundational facet of schooling. Culture provides windows that help us to observe and think about how and why people organize life on a day-to-day basis, and culture traverses the school gate every day (Lee et al., 2020). In addition to this, we should speak in the plural, as people are simultaneously involved in a diverse array of cultural milieus requiring ongoing negotiation of the constraints and possibilities associated with each of these (Lee et al., 2020). In other words, schooling is experienced in and through many cultural and linguistic frameworks.

Further underpinning the salience of emphasizing genuine and deep engagement with cultural pluralism, we can reflect on changes within schooling over the last fifty-plus years. The post-civil rights era led to increased movements of people around the world, changing the demographics of learners in schools in many national settings. Associated with these changes, education policies, curriculum/pedagogy, and research initiatives have worked towards responding to the shifting and dynamic cultural contexts of schooling (Inglis, 2009). In the Australian setting, since the 1980s, this has been dominated by thinking and practices falling under discourses of multiculturalism and/or inclusion (Watkins & Noble, 2019). In the effort not to go off at a tangent, given ongoing concerns with achievement standards for some culturally and linguistically diverse groups, perhaps we can proceed with accepting that the ambitions of these initiatives have fallen short for many students, parents, and communities (Anderson & Boyle, 2019). I use the word many, as of course there are also examples that are a lot more encouraging.

One of these more encouraging directions calls for everyday engagement with the cultural resources that learners arrive at school with. Alim and Paris (2017) refer to the umbrella term *asset-based* pedagogies for these approaches – it is also described in terms of adopting cultural wealth frameworks for schooling. In their words:

> These revolutionary pedagogies repositioned the linguistic, literate, and cultural practices of working-class communities – specifically poor communities of color – as resources and assets to honor, explore, and extend in accessing White middle-class dominant cultural norms of acting and being that are demanded in schools. (p. 4)

An umbrella term is necessary because there has been a dizzying array of terminology used since the roots of this education field emerged in the 1970s (Morrison et al., 2019). For example, influential research emerged following on from Moll and colleagues' (1992) conceptualization of 'funds of knowledges'. There is also the culturally responsive framing from Gay (2010) and culturally relevant teaching from Ladson-Billings (1995), and, more recently, culturally sustaining schooling outlined by Paris (2012), which all make widely noted contributions to this field. In common, asset-based pedagogies work from the understanding that all students arrive at the school gate already knowledgeable and capable in a variety of ways, and it is the responsibility of educators to learn from and with students in ways that meaningfully flow into teaching and learning. When genuinely undertaken, asset-based approaches should not be viewed in superficial and simplistic ways as a device that hook students into lessons, with traditional teaching and learning patterns then reasserted.

The approaches just mentioned could be expanded on. However, outlining the scope and significance of scholarship and schooling practices that take up asset-based approaches is beyond the purview of this Element. Rather, the suggestion being advanced is the potential for punk scholarship and skooling practices to learn from and with this field. And this is because asset-based approaches value and meaningfully work with the cultural and linguistic resources that students, families, and communities share as a cornerstone of better addressing inequities and discrimination in schooling. In this sense, and importantly, the mobilization of asset-based pedagogies are embraced with a view to improving the educational experiences of students who have been 'marginalized by systemic inequalities based on race, ethnicity, and language' (Paris, 2012, p. 93) – and we could add those who experience discrimination regarding gender, sex, religion, class, and so on. Hence, asset-based approaches contribute to ameliorating the harms and violence that stem from the dominant culture in the form of deficit approaches to schooling that have long influenced the sector (p. 93). And as has been noted by Ladson-Billings (2014, p. 76), when improving schooling for those who have traditionally not been well served by it, improvements and positive change are concurrently experienced by all students.

Instead of detracting from this body of work, it may be helpful to further explore how and why punk may serve to constructively contribute by adding to critiques of dominant schooling practices. Hence, there is much to agree with in the view from Santos and Guerra (2018):

> we argue that punk has a critical role to play in the theory and practice of education as it enables and reiterates a critical opposition to the status quo, permitting multiple resistance stances and contributing counterhegemonic voice through its informal and de-centralised networks and activities. (p. 211)

While Ladson-Billings (2014) has been advancing this field since the 1990s, recently her attention turned more directly to consider how and why these efforts have also fallen short of their ambitions. In her words, she has grown 'increasingly dissatisfied' with the rigid and superficial ways that culture has understood and engaged with teaching and learning (p. 77). This is particularly the case in relation to the sociopolitical dimensions of schooling practices that continue to fall short of critically engaging with 'policies and practices that may have direct impact' on the lives of students and communities (p. 78). Said another way, many educators have taken up thin or weak versions of asset-based approaches by failing to seriously consider the complexity, fluidity, and significance of teaching and learning in culturally and linguistically conscious ways.

Cultures shift and change over time, and hence culture should not be understood as static or rigid. The logic following on from this is that pedagogical theorizing and practices also need to be dynamic, and so it should come as little surprise that leaders in the field such as Ladson-Billings (2014) are illustrative of this. As she details in her paper about the 'remix' of her own pedagogical practices that evolved by learning with and from students in teacher education: 'I depended on them to lead me to consider new ways of understanding how popular culture can be deployed to engage in conversations about critical theoretical concepts such as hegemony, audit cultures, and neoliberalism as well as to develop new pedagogical strategies' (p. 79). These efforts led Ladson-Billings (2018) to engage meaningfully with cultural and linguistic assets linked with hip hop to 'r(e)volutionize' her approach to education. The notion of remixing from Ladson-Billings (2014) also resonates with the ideas in Section 3 about turning over the compost, as it invites thinking about drawing on what is already known, familiar, and in-place to breathe new life in ways that are generative and enriching.

There are synergies between hip hop and punk that have been noted by others. Schwartz and Robertson (2018) observe that punk and hip hop share equally long and somewhat intertwined histories. Smith (2020, p. 112) also addresses the intersections of punk and hip hop, suggesting they are 'both excellent *agent provocateurs*. They prompt, prod, provoke and they prevail' (original emphasis). Indeed, to further illustrate this point, Smith draws on punk pedagogical frameworks to analyse a collection of songs from hip hop artists. Smith (2020) is seemingly motivated by the potential for hip hop to assist with interrogating issues of race and racism. For those who grew up with hip hop such as Love (2014, p. 53), her 'understanding of the world is rooted in hip hop culture' which provided an education that helped with better understanding the racialized injustices of the worlds she moved through, and taught her lessons about developing critical voices that enable acting on and in the world in ways to address socioeconomic and political inequities. In common, both punk and hip hop can be understood and engaged with as cultivating cultural (and hence political) consciousness. However, both punk and hip hop have also been haunted by the lure and domestication that comes with commercial success, and advocates of hip hop pedagogies remain wary of ways that cultural assets can be 'stolen, repackaged and sold back' to communities in ways that reproduce inequities (Emdin, 2018).

Schwartz and Robertson (2018, p. 140) describe hip hop and punk as movements with the potential to help transform education. They combine humour, political critique, and activism in ways that foster agency and empowerment in the lives of students. Following on from these lines of thinking, we can observe that punk and hip hop offer a constellation of cultural and linguistic assets that can be drawn on in ways that assist teaching and learning. Moreover, it seems to me that in the work of those advocating hip hop approaches for education we can also observe the punk sensibilities articulated by Way (2021). There is a commitment to the import of creating and caring for community; being subversive in productive and generative ways; actively working towards sociopolitical consciousness; and people know that they can't wait around for things to get done for them. Both punk and hip hop are also a reflection of and continue to share foundational relationships with the dominant culture, hence they help reveal aspects of dominant culture that are harmful and reproduce injustices. Given that both punk and hip hop pedagogies are grounded in concerns such as those to do with power, voice, and representation, the influences of Freire and critical pedagogies often trace through this work.

While it is interesting to consider the connections between punk and hip hop, I want to conclude this subsection by returning to some of the earlier discussion. Hip hop pedagogies derive from a large and long-established field of pedagogical theorizing and research that is founded on asset-based approaches to teaching and learning. To date, contributions to the emerging field of punk pedagogies have not seemingly sought to conceptualize how and why it could also draw on this broader body of literature and schooling practices. At the very least, attention is not directed towards these lines of thinking in foundational texts such as Torrez (2012), Dines (2015a), the 'brief history' of punk pedagogies in the introduction to Smith and colleagues (2018), nor the introduction from the more recent text from Stewart and Way (2023). I would contend that this is a potentially rich and worthwhile line of thinking that warrants further consideration.

4.5 Punk and Critical Consciousness: Learning to Act On and In the World

As with others concerned with pedagogical and curriculum theorizing (see Watkins & Noble, 2019), Ladson-Billings (2018) suggests that culture remains one of the most misunderstood concepts engaged with in asset-based approaches. This itself is worrying; however, while culture (in general) and cultural consciousness (in particular) continues to be confusing, it is attending meaningfully to sociopolitical (or critical) consciousness which is the most ignored facet of this work (p. 23). As she goes on to outline, fostering sociopolitical consciousness can be thought of as an approach to teaching and learning that actively encourages and opens up possibilities for students to 'question the veracity of what they read in classrooms and pose powerful questions about social, cultural, economic, political, and other problems of living in a democracy that attempts to serve a diverse populace' (p. 23). At stake is fostering the skill, understanding, and motivation to act on and in the world.

For Freire (2013, p. 45), culture itself is a significant touchstone for teaching and learning, and more to the point, cultural literacy entails developing 'an attitude of creation and re-creation, a self-transformation producing a stance of intervention in one's own context'. In contrast to this, and with the worry gestured to by Ladson-Billings (2018), it is perhaps more common for simplistic and celebratory engagement with culture to be used in schooling as a way of making schooling appear more welcoming, safe, familiar, and accessible, and thus the sociopolitical conscious-raising opportunities are passed over altogether. While noting that schooling should of course be welcoming, safe, familiar, and accessible, if there is little attention directed to addressing the structural arrangements and practices that maintain social injustices and inequities, then it seems unlikely there will be any meaningful or sustainable change to the schooling experiences of many.

In the case of Australia, this is observable with changes connected to engaging with Aboriginal and Torres Strait Islander cultural heritage and knowledges in schooling. If I think back to when I was a primary school student starting in 1979, I would now describe those days as being unapologetically violent towards and about First Nations heritage and knowledge systems – it was a White-washed narrative that largely relied on and reproduced stereotypical representations and understandings of people, history, and knowledges. Perhaps it is worth the reminder that it was only in the 1970s that the White Australia policy was formally abolished; settings such as NSW moved away from the 'clean, clad and courteous' policies that enabled the exclusion of Aboriginal and Torres Strait Islander students from education; and federal policies were introduced to engage and involve these communities (Soutphommasane & Low, 2023).

While there were some encouraging changes twenty-five years later, as a high school teacher it appeared to me that efforts were typically a thin veneer that students likely saw through. For example, in the library there were spears, boomerangs, and other artefacts that represented Aboriginal and Torres Strait Islander cultural heritage; however, nobody was able to offer any explanations of where they came from, why they were there, or the stories they related to. I also still remember several of the English classrooms having posters lining the walls that depicted the book spines, titles, and authors of so-called classics – the bread and butter of the English canon. However, the authors were overwhelmingly identifiable as White, male, English-speaking voices, with a handful of titles that likely were well in the sights of Said (2019 [1978]) when he critically unpacked the makings of Orientalism in the 1970s.

On a related note, observing disrespectful responses from colleagues during professional learning activities about education policy changes concerning Aboriginal and Torres Strait Islander academic achievements – linked with the emergence of national testing – prompted me to undertake research for my PhD. My study investigated the role and contribution of teachers as race-makers in the classroom, and in doing so led me to engage with asset-based pedagogical theorizing (see Vass 2016, 2017).

Now, as an education researcher when visiting schools, it is relatively standard practice to see Aboriginal and Torres Strait Islander flags waving, the National Apology[24] framed in the front office, a Welcome or Acknowledgement to Country to begin formal school proceedings, events such as NAIDOC[25] day in the school calendar, attention directed to 'closing achievement gaps', and

---

[24] In 2008 Prime Minister Kevin Rudd presented a formal apology to Aboriginal and Torres Strait Islander Peoples. For more on this see www.aph.gov.au/Visit_Parliament/Art/Exhibitions/Custom_Media/Apology_to_Australias_Indigenous_Peoples.

[25] The National Aborigines and Islanders Day Observance Committee (NAIDOC) has links that reach back to protest movement efforts from the 1920s, and was formally supported as a day of remembrance. For more about NAIDOC, see www.naidoc.org.au/about/history.

evidence of cross-curricular inclusion of knowledges, histories, and perspectives in teaching and learning. On the surface much has changed, but how much has this all meaningfully impacted on the schooling experiences and sociopolitical consciousness of learners in classrooms since it all began in the 1970s?

If the recent results in the 2023 national Referendum are anything to go by, it indicates that many people around the country still have a lot to address in their collective sociopolitical consciousness and relationships with the First Peoples of Australia. The Referendum sought to make constitutional change that would enable Aboriginal and Torres Strait Islander Peoples to have representative body to speak directly with the Federal government on issues that impacted on them. This proposal was arguably a very modest change, but it was rejected around the nation – in the state of Queensland where I live and work, nearly 70% of the votes were 'no'.[26] This outcome raises serious questions about the role, contribution, and purposes of education from a historical perspective and also for the future.

To reiterate, efforts to make schooling more welcoming, safe, familiar, and accessible are of course important, and not attending to these concerns is actively problematic. But on their own they are insufficient for meaningful change to occur if the core business of teaching, learning, and assessment remains unchanged. If we do not explicitly and meaningfully interrogate the dominant sociopolitical milieu that shapes the worlds we inhabit, it seems quite likely (at least to me) that over time, there is the potential for learners to see through the façade and to question what relevance schooling has for them and the worlds they move through. In these circumstances, it is the absence of attending to the sociopolitical consciousness of *all* learners (and educators) that is significant, as it is this dimension that makes teaching and learning personally meaningful.

In essence, this is an underlying theme exposed in the research about non-formal learning pathways by Cordova (2017). For the participants in her study, the growing awareness of the 'mis-education' offered in schooling, when coupled with the absence of meaningful support connected with the self-concept of learners, led those involved to engage with punk as a form of educative 'healing'. This too resonates with the experiences of Torrez (2012) as a young person who encountered punk beyond the boundaries of school and found: 'For once, my questions did not raise eyebrows or stop a conversation in its discursive tracks. What an energising feeling to be part of a conversation, rather than simply the receiving end of a whispered conversation' (p. 132).

---

[26] For some of the initial responses to the outcome, see www.sbs.com.au/nitv/article/tonight-is-not-the-end-of-the-road-australians-react-to-news-of-defeated-referendum/gsnzbjtv0.

Aspects of this also resonate with my movement from secondary schooling into the world beyond. As I have written about elsewhere, it was bands such as TISM (This is Serious Mum) that offered irreverent and critical sociopolitical commentary that came to be influential for me in the early 1990s (Vass, 2023). Like others I found the satire in the cultural production of punk opening up knowledge-making (learning) opportunities as the lyrics, performances, recordings, art, style, and so on were an invitation for participants to be contributors to the processes of cultural production in a way that 'resists codification' (Schwartz & Robertson, 2018, p. 129). More recent contributions from bands such as The Chats, whom I was introduced to by my nephew, continue in this vein, as they are illustrative of a stripped back and laconic approach that offers satirical sociopolitical commentary that provokes thinking.

While it was their 2017 song 'Smoko' that elevated the band to international attention, by 2019 The Chats were offering songs such as 'I hope Scott's house burns down' that humorously derided the then Australian prime minister. The song offered commentary about a family holiday to a Pacific Island by the political leader, while hugely destructive fires were causing environmental and community devastation in parts of Australia (see Vass, 2023). While the lyrics, artwork, and style of punk such as this offer thought-provoking content, there is more to think about and be learnt from genuinely engaging with punk sensibilities and cultural production – the balance of content and form are significant (Dines, 2015b). Moreover, as Schwartz (2015) encourages, the 'rebellion' underpinning punk cultural production should not deflect attention from the ways this establishes 'alternative educational spaces' that are infused with political and philosophic creativity. The broader point is to provoke thinking about knowledge-making practices, active and informed citizenship, and thinking critically about the worlds we are making and moving through. And this, is – or at least should be – more central to what takes place in formal school settings than sometimes seems to be the case.

There will always be debate regarding the qualities and merits of different punk bands, songs, scenes – this provides people with a lot to talk about when they catch up and should not be considered as undermining punk (Kwiatek, 2022). So, for some, bands such as TISM or The Chats may not be viewed as being quite punk enough. However, it seems to me that efforts to assert boundaries and rules regarding punk are akin to the sort of constraints and control imposed by mainstream schooling that most (if not all) punks aim to critique. In the case of schooling, the curriculum looms large here, and education and many educators remain heavily invested in protecting knowledge-making practices that preserve the prestige, legitimacy, and authority of the scientific method, English canon, high art, the base-10 system, and White-washed historiography (see Apple, 2019; Deng, 2020).

To be honest, I suspect that most of us – as educators – do it to varying degrees and with different slants, but whichever way you cut it, little everyday moments in formal school settings contribute to upholding knowledge-making hierarchies of this ilk. For example, as a history teacher I can reflect on how and why it is hard to avoid potentially elevating the visibility and value that is placed on 'evidence' that is written or visual, at the expense of oral or grassroot level contributions to historical investigations. Similarly, I have observed the best-of-intentioned science teachers who may actively try to be critical by interrupting dominant knowledge-making practices, but who nonetheless recentre the scientific method as the most legitimate and authoritative approach to generating knowledges connected to the field of science. And questions about math as being culture or value free, challenging its assumed objectivity, or drawing attention to the ways that the base-10 system came to dominate the world as implicated in ongoing processes of colonialism, has seemingly been a stretch too far on occasions.

Said another way, while history, science, and math (or any) curriculum and assessment remain yoked to knowledge-making practices that are implicated in preserving the colonial matrix of power (Mignolo, 2007), little is likely to change. Moreover, to do otherwise requires the sort of vigilance that is seemingly impossible to maintain, particularly in the neoliberal-infused accountability era discussed previously. The follow-on effects are the reproduction of structural arrangements that underpin social injustices and inequities in the worlds we move through outside of formal educational settings (Bourdieu & Passeron, 1977).

As already observed, it is with a view to these lines of thinking that the influences of Freire and critical pedagogies have been taken up in punk (Parkinson, 2017, p. 145). Having said this, Parkinson (2017) adroitly unpacks concerns to do with this approach, which are well worth heeding. The first of these is to do with attending purposefully to a key touchstone of punk, namely, that diversity within and across the movement (or scenes) is quintessential. Punk is temporal- and locality-specific, with those involved responsive to the particularities of context. The second concern, which in some respects is linked with or may flow out of the first, is to do with whether or not those who have not engaged meaningfully with punk in their personal lives can or even should attempt this in their professional life as educators.

Sharing similar concerns that point in this direction, Bestley (2018, p. 18) is wary of the potential for educators to rely on stereotypical punk aesthetics and concepts that fall short of critically understanding the contexts and politics that underpin the creation and sharing of cultural resources in the first place. There is crossover again with hip hop, and lessons on offer by engaging with texts such as Greenfield (2007), a self-identified 'white middle-age guy teaching hip hop'. He shares his experiences about the import of deep and genuine interrogation of our 'cultural frames of reference' when drawing on cultural and linguistic resources that are not part of our socialization and identity-work. Emdin (2016) recently offered a collection of provocations that aim to support the efforts of 'white folks who teach in the hood'. The goal he encourages moving towards is for any and every educator, irrespective where they happen to be teaching, to be more culturally and politically nuanced with how they understand and approach the purposes and practices of schooling.

It is hard to disagree with these cautionary tales; however, here too I think that there are lessons to be learnt from other asset-based approaches. For example, Ladson-Billings (2009) reminds us that teachers can and should meaningfully learn about the cultural worlds of students' lives that may differ from their own. And importantly, when they do so, the teachers are a lot more effective in the classroom. So, in drawing this section to an end, please keep in mind that the ideas being advanced are not suggesting that teachers need to try and become or think of themselves as punk, nor are they being encouraged take up teaching and learning practices that result in classrooms full of students that think of or describe themselves as punks. While this poses an interesting thought-experiment, it would ultimately be missing the point.

Instead, the ambition has been to encourage consideration of the import of working with young learners in the classroom in ways that identity-work (which they are doing regardless of your efforts as a teacher) fosters capacities and reasons to later act on and in the world in ways that can address the many social, economic, political, environmental, and technological challenges ahead of them. It is therefore about encouraging asset-based approaches to punk pedagogies that place less emphasis on content, and instead prioritize process in connection with skooling. This is about building on – or redirecting – our efforts to enact teaching and learning about the 'culture of power', as Delpit (2011) describes it, which opens up pathways later in life to navigate and benefit from the structural arrangements we all move through. While there may still be scope and reasoning for making this explicit, rather than accepting and graciously submitting to the longevity of the dominant 'culture of power' that emerged as part of the project of modernity, wouldn't it be transformative to work with learners in ways that they can envisage and believe in as hopefully changing the structural arrangements that protect the status quo?

5 Punk, Hope, and the Restorative Potential of Skooling

Punk pedagogy is a manifestation of equity, rebellion, critique, self-examination, solidarity, community, love, anger, and collaboration. It is a space where the teacher–learner hierarchy is disavowed and the normative discourse of traditional teaching is dissembled.

(Torrez, 2012, p. 136)

If part of the punk sensibilities that emerged in the 1970s included a rejection of the excess, indulgence, and commodification of dominant (or popular) culture, one of the hallmarks of this was the creation of relatively short and sharp songs that didn't rely on overly complex chord progressions or layering of sounds. Kreider (2022, p. 289) describes this in terms of *aesthetic anarchy* – the aim was 'less complexity and order and more simplicity and chaos'. So, while the text you are reading is likely already longer than it should be in this spirit, hopefully it has worked towards this aesthetic by not presenting overly complex or layered ideas. I would hope that there has been a simplicity in terms of engaging with the text, albeit accepting that at times it may have seemed a bit on the chaotic side.

In a nutshell, and to restate the point, identity matters, and we know that it matters. With a simmering line of questioning that follows on from this, we can ask if more of the same in schooling will lead to better or different outcomes for students who are currently not well served by education? Hence, we can consider if there are grounds to think about supporting identity-work in more innovative and creative ways than may currently be the case for many students. Culture matters, and we also know that it matters. It is cultural practices that establish the sense of insiderness and outsiderness that people experience and internalize, influencing the ways we (re)story our sense of self. And with the dominant culture imbued with the influences of consumption, competition, and individualism, which are located within contexts that are experiencing increasing inequities, there are seemingly more of us on the outside than on the inside.

Hence, we can ask if there are ways we can utilize cultural resources that are critical of dominant culture in support of meaningfully interrogating the construction of knowledges in the classroom. For me, in an effort to connect with the voices of others, I find much to agree with the suggestion that punk sensibilities matter, as they make available the cultural resources that are well suited to this undertaking. Which invites the question: what do you think now? Are you starting to imagine ways that punk sensibilities may help you with transforming teaching and learning?

An expression that I often find myself drawn to sharing with educators runs along these lines: if we want to produce different outcomes in education, then we need to do things differently in skool. I can't remember where I came across this idea or who I learnt it from, but the sentiment has always been underpinned by an understanding that the industrial model of formal schooling that was largely designed by European thinkers and established around the world has passed its use-by date. It is the model of 'education' that is so very familiar that if you close your eyes and think of words like school, classroom, teacher, or student, images will easily come to mind that are not too dissimilar anywhere you travel in the world. It is not just educational settings that appear similar; the notions of teaching, learning, and assessment are too, resulting in recognizable activities and practices that are typically associated with 'education'. And then of course there are the goals and purposes for which young people are expected to attend these settings – to be socialized and foster the skills and knowledges that will later allow them to meaningfully contribute to the world as adults through employment of some type (Cote, 2014). It is so familiar. Why would anyone want to do things differently? What does it even mean, to do things differently?

Over the last few years, I have had the opportunity to work with people such as Gamilaroi scholar Michelle Bishop, who has frequently reminded me that the education system is working as it was designed – as a tool of colonialism that was established to reward a privileged few, discipline the majority into compliance and conformity, and to impart on everybody the notion that that the world is available for exploitation and extraction in the service of humanity. Her work in this space is currently pursuing what may be possible if schooling is reimagined with what she is describing as *education sovereignty* (Bishop, 2022). In part, this starts with accepting that *education* (the version that is about being immersed in knowledge-making practices) has been happening in Australia for more years than is easily comprehensible. As Bishop (2022) outlines:

> Knowledge has been exchanged for thousands of generations, ensuring continued sustenance and abundance for people, Country and the more-than-human. *Living, thriving, creating, nurturing.* So, what if we decided to look to our old ways and started to 'do' education on our own terms? For all students, grounded in Indigenous ways. What would that look and feel like? (p. 136, original italics)

For Bishop, as with the work of those she is inspired by and draws on, the foundations on which schooling itself has been designed and operates requires urgent rethinking about reimagining what formal education could or should be for future generations. So, as she has reminded me on occasion, unfortunately there are many involved in education who may not really want to do schooling differently. But I remain hopeful – and I suspect she does too!

As was noted earlier, my experiences as a student and then as a teacher serve as a reminder that there are many students who see the education system for what it is. Indeed, in a similar line of thinking Tuck and Yang (2014, p. 2) make the point that over a great many years young people have actively resisted educational injustices and have conveyed this message in eclectic, defiant, and at times creative ways. However, rejecting school in the form of literally leaving it remains common and widespread, which is a poor outcome. But for those who remain there are 'significant costs for those students who stay in demeaning schools' (Tuck & Yang, 2014, p. 2) –which is also a poor outcome. Is there more that we can do as educators to advocate and work in support of the resistance that students communicate, rather than trying to contain or extinguish these responses to dominant culture?

One of my reasons for referring to the work of Bishop (2022) is because it gestures to the hopeful and restorative potential of skooling to look, sound, feel, and be practiced in ways that are very different from the status quo. In essence, for me it is an approach that epitomizes the idea of doing things differently, with a view to producing different outcomes. I doubt Bishop would describe this approach as punk, but where there may be a point of similarity with some of the ideas being explored across this Element is the sense that cultural and linguistic resources and artefacts that come from beyond dominant culture can be drawn on in ways that transform education. Moreover, Bishop's work invites thinking about the identities of learners in school settings in ways that may deviate some distance from what is currently experienced. As such, it is also important to note that the thinking and work of Bishop differs in the sense that it centres learning on, from, and with Country.[27]

For some of you, there may be an appealing rationale in thinking about transforming teaching and learning by drawing on Country. Indeed, my years of research and teaching have drawn attention to ways that many educators articulate support regarding the import of centring Country in education – or at the least of more genuinely and meaningfully including Indigenous knowledges, histories, and perspectives. However, this also often foregrounds concerns with confidence, familiarity, and questions about accessing suitable resources and then drawing on these in educational settings (Craven, Yeung & Han, 2014). In contrast with the uncertainty that many non-Indigenous educators

---

[27] 'Country' with a capital 'C' is an Aboriginal English term. Bawaka Country and colleagues (2015, p. 274) explain that 'People, including researchers, are made through Country, they are part of Country and Country is part of them. We all come into existence through relationships with each other and with the world itself. Hence, Country directs attention to the significance of the lands, waterways, skies, and more-than-human elements of the natural world, from which humans are not separate.'

may experience in connection with meaningfully learning from and with Country, it is because punk shares a relationship with the cultural and linguistic resources associated with dominant culture that it seems likely that there may be more familiarity – and from this confidence – with drawing on punk sensibilities for skooling. And, as I have been arguing, punk sensibilities are also able to offer hope for the efforts of educators who seek to transform teaching and learning in ways that reignite the restorative potential of skooling.

The quote that opens this final section, from Torrez (2012), is illustrative of the inspired, evocative, and provocative challenge laid down by advocates of punk sensibilities. It is a quote befitting bringing this Element to a close – for me it is akin to a microphone-dropping moment and kicking over the drum-kit. It also gestures to the four punk sensibilities outlined by Way (2021). First, it is now time for greater numbers of educators to establish teaching and learning communities in which the identities of individuals are nurtured relationally and are intertwined with those of the broader social milieu. Second, the harmful and constraining practices of dominant culture can and should be interrupted and subverted to serve the more-than-human world that people are part of and reliant on. Third, as a matter of urgency, teaching and learning must work towards fostering sociopolitical consciousness to empower people to act on and in the world in ways that address the legacies of the colonial epoch. And lastly, it is in and through adopting DIY approaches to getting things done that may produce different outcomes in and from schooling – and, as anybody that has worked in a school knows, it is not as if anybody is going to turn up any time soon to do it for us.

References

Alim, H. & Paris, D. (2017). What is culturally sustaining pedagogy and why does it matter? In Paris, D. & Alim, H. (Eds.). *Culturally sustaining pedagogies: Teaching and learning for justice in a changing world* (pp. 1–21). New York: Teachers College.

Anderson, J. & Boyle, C. (2019). Looking in the mirror: Reflecting on 25 years of inclusive education in Australia. *International Journal of Inclusive Education, 23*(7–8), 796–810.

Apple, M. (2019). *Ideology and curriculum* (4th ed.). New York: Routledge.

Au, W. (2012). *Critical curriculum studies: Education, consciousness, and the politics of knowing.* New York: Routledge.

Ball, S. (2016). Subjectivity as a site of struggle: Refusing neoliberalism? *British Journal of Sociology of Education, 37*(8), 1129–1146.

Bawaka Country, Wright, S., Suchet-Pearson, S., Lloyd, K., Burarrwanga, L., Ganambarr, R., Ganambarr-Stubbs, M., Ganambarr, B. & Maymuru, D. (2015). Working with learning from Country: Decentring human author-ity. *Cultural Geographies, 22*(2), 269–283.

Beer, D. (2014). *Punk sociology.* New York: Palgrave Macmillan.

Bell, A. & Ream, R. (2021). Troubling Pākehā relations to place: Composting home stories. *Departures in Critical Qualitative Research, 10*(1), 97–116.

Bennett, A. & Guerra, P. (2018). Rethinking DIY culture in a post-industrial and global context. In Bennett, A. & Guerra, P. (Eds.). *DIY cultures and underground music scenes* (pp. 7–18). London: Routledge.

Berlant, L. (2011). *Cruel optimism.* Durham: Duke University Press.

Bestley, R. (2018). Art attacks: Punk methods and design education. In Dylan, G., Dines, M. & Parkinson, T. (Eds.). *Punk pedagogies: Music, culture and learning* (pp. 13–29). New York: Routledge.

Bestley, R., Dines, M., Gordon, A. & Guerra, P. (2019). Introduction: The punk narrative turned upside down: Research transmissions from the local to the global. In Bestley, R., Dines, M., Gordon, A. & Guerra, P. (Eds.). *The punk reader: Research transmissions from the local and the global* (pp. 9–26). Bristol: Intellect.

Bestley, R., Dines, M. & Stewart, F. (2023). A network of hardcore researchers: Punk studies, punk scholarship, punk pedagogy. In Butz, K. & Winkler, R. (Eds.) *Hardcore research: Punk, practice, politics* (pp. 45–60). Bielefeld: Transcript Verlag.

Bestley, R. & Ogg, A. (2022). *The art of punk: Posters + Flyers + Fanzines + Record Sleeves.* London: Omnibus Press.

Bishop, M. (2022). Indigenous education sovereignty: Another way of 'doing' education. *Critical Studies in Education, 63*(1), 131–146.

Bourdieu, P. & Passeron, J. (1977). *Reproduction in education, society and culture.* London: Sage.

Brown, T. (2015). Teachers on film. In Jubas, K., Taber, N. & Brown, T. (Eds.). *Popular culture as pedagogy: Research in the field of adult education* (pp. 49–66). Rotterdam: Sense Publishers.

Chapman, T. & Hobbel, N. (2022). Introduction: Conversations, problems, and action. In Chapman, T. & Hobbel, N. (Eds.). *Social justice pedagogy across the curriculum: The practice of freedom* (2nd ed., pp. 1–6). New York: Routledge.

Cochran-Smith, M., Carney, M. & Keefe, E., et al. (2018). *Reclaiming accountability in teacher education.* New York: Teachers College Press.

Collins, P. & Bilge, S. (2016). *Intersectionality.* Cambridge: Polity.

Connell, R. (2013). The neoliberal cascade and education: An essay on the market agenda and its consequences. *Critical Studies in Education, 54*(2), 99–112.

Cordova, R. (2017). *DIY Punk as education: From mis-education to educative healing.* Charlotte: Information Age.

Cote, J. (2014). *Youth studies: Fundamental issues and debates.* Basingstoke: Palgrave Macmillan.

Craven, R., Yeung, A. & Han, F. (2014). The impact of professional development and Indigenous education officers on Australian teachers' Indigenous teaching and learning. *Australian Journal of Teacher Education, 39*(8), 85–108.

Crenshaw, K. (1991). Mapping the margins: Intersectionality, identity politics, and violence against women of color. *Stanford Law Review, 43*(6), 1241–1300.

Dale, P. (2016). *Anyone can do it: Empowerment, tradition and the punk underground.* Abingdon: Routledge.

Delpit. L. (2011). The silenced dialogue: Power and pedagogy in educating other peoples' children. In Hilty, E. (ed.). *Thinking about schools: A foundation of education reader* (pp. 157–175). Boulder: Westview.

Deng, Z. (2020). *Knowledge, content, curriculum and didaktik: Beyond social realism.* Abingdon: Routledge.

Dines, M. (2015a). Learning through resistance: Contextualisation, creation and incorporation of a 'punk pedagogy'. *Journal of Pedagogic Development, 5* (3), 20–31.

Dines, M. (2015b). Reflections on the peripheral: Punk, pedagogy, and the domestication of the radical. *Punk & Post-Punk, 4*(2&3), 129–140.

Dines, M. (2023). Learning on the road: Stonehenge, skool bus, and the development of alternative pedagogies in the new age traveller movement of the 1980s. In Stewart, F. & Way, L. (Eds.). *Punk pedagogies in practice: Disruptions and connections* (pp. 144–159). Bristol: Intellect.

Donaghey, J. & Prasetyo, F. (2021). Punk space in Bandung, Indonesia: Evasion and confrontation. In Bestley, R., Dines, M., Gordon, A. & Guerra, P. (Eds.). *Trans-global punk scenes: The punk reader vol. 2* (pp. 137–161). Bristol: Intellect.

Dunn, K. (2012). 'If it ain't cheap, it ain't punk': Walter Benjamin's progressive cultural production and DIY punk record labels. *Journal of Popular Music Studies, 24*(2), 217–237.

Dunn, K. (2016). *Global punk: Resistance and rebellion in everyday life.* New York: Bloomsbury.

Egeberg, H., McConney, A. & Price, A. (2021). Teachers' views on effective classroom management: A mixed-methods investigation in Western Australian high schools. *Educational Research for Policy and Practice, 20*, 107–124.

Elliott, A. (2016). *Identity troubles: An introduction.* Abingdon: Routledge.

Emdin, C. (2016). *For white folks who teach in the hood . . . and all the rest of y'all too: Reality pedagogy and urban education.* Boston: Beacon.

Emdin, C. (2018). Introduction. In Emdin, C. & Adjapong, E. (Eds.). *# HipHopEd: The compilation on hip hop education* (pp. 1–11). Leiden: Brill.

Francis, B., Taylor, B. & Tereshchenko, A. (2020). *Reassessing 'ability' grouping: Improving practice for equity and attainment.* Abingdon: Routledge.

Freire, P. (1996). *Pedagogy of the oppressed.* London: Penguin.

Freire, P. (2013). *Education for critical consciousness.* London: Bloomsbury.

Furness, Z. (Ed.). (2012). *Punkademics: The basement show in the ivory tower.* Brooklyn: Autonomedia.

Gay, G. (2010). *Culturally responsive teaching: Theory, research, and practice.* New York: Teachers College Press.

Gaztambide-Fernández, R. & Rose, L. (2015). Social justice and urban music education. In Benedict, C., Schmidt, P., Spruce, G. & Woodford, P. (Eds.). *The Oxford handbook of social justice in music education* (pp. 456–472). New York: Oxford University Press.

Gibbs, K. & McKay, L. (2021). Differentiated teaching practices of Australian mainstream classroom teachers: A systematic review and thematic analysis. *International Journal of Educational Research, 109*, pp. 1–9.

Gobby, B. & Millei, Z. (2022). A history of schooling and the making of children. In Gobby, B. & Walker, R. (Eds.). *Powers of curriculum: Sociological aspects of education* (2nd ed., pp. 42–61). Victoria: Oxford University Press.

Green, B. (2019). Whose riot? Collective memory of an iconic event in a local music scene. *Journal of Sociology, 55*(1), 144–160.

Greenfield, D. (2007). What's the deal with the white middle-age guy teaching hip hop? Lessons in popular culture, positionality and pedagogy. *Pedagogy, Culture & Society, 15*(2), 229–243.

Habell-Pallán, M. (2005). '¿Soy Punkera, Y Que?': Sexuality, translocality, and punk in Los Angeles and beyond. In Tadiar, N. X. M. & Davis, A. Y. (Eds.). *Beyond the frame: Women of colour and visual representation* (pp. 219–242). New York: Palgrave Macmillan.

Haenfler, R. (2006). *Straight edge: Hardcore punk, clean living youth, and social change*. New Brunswick: Rutgers.

Hall, S. (2000). Who needs 'identity'? In Du Gay, P., Evans, J. & Redman, P. (Eds.). *Identity: A reader* (pp. 15–30). London: Sage.

Hamilton, J. & Neimanis, A. (2018). Composting feminisms and environmental humanities. *Environmental Humanities, 10*(2), 502–527.

Haraway, D. (2015). Anthropocene, Capitalocene, Plantationocene, Chthulucene: Making kin. *Environmental Humanities, 6*(1), 159–165.

Haraway, D. (2016). *Staying with the trouble: Making kin in the Chthulucene*. Durham: Duke University Press.

Hayes, D., Mills, M., Christie, P. & Lingard, B. (2006). *Teachers & schooling making a difference: Productive pedagogies, assessment and performance*. Crows Nest: Allen & Unwin.

Heffernan, A., Longmuir, F., Bright, D. & Kim, M. (2019). *Perceptions of teachers and teaching in Australia*. Melbourne: Monash University.

Hesmondalgh, D. (2008). Cultural and creative industries. In Bennett, T. & Frow, J. (Eds.). *The SAGE handbook of cultural analysis* (pp. 552–569). London: Sage.

Hess, J. (2019). *Music education for social change: Constructing an activist music education*. New York: Routledge.

hooks, b. (2003). *Teaching community: A pedagogy of hope*. New York: Routledge.

Hounslow-Eyre, A. (2023). The future is unwritten: Joe Strummer, prophetic pedagogy, and complexity as resistance. In Stewart, F. & Way, L. (Eds.). *Punk pedagogies in practice: Disruptions and connections* (pp.27–45). Bristol: Intellect.

Inglis, C. (2009). Multicultural education in Australia: Two generations of evolution. In Banks, J. (Ed.). *The Routledge companion to multicultural education* (pp. 109–120). New York: Routledge.

Johnston, O. & Taylor, B. (2023). A systematic literature review of between-class ability groupings in Australia: Enduring tensions, new directions. *Issues in Educational Research, 22*(1), 91–117.

Jones, E. (2021). DIY and popular music: Mapping an ambivalent relationship across three historical case studies. *Popular Music and Society, 44*(1), 60–78.

Kaeding, T. (2007). *(I'm) Stranded by the Saints*. National Film and Sound Archive of Australia. Retrieved 12 July 2021 from www.nfsa.gov.au/collec tion/curated/im-stranded-saints.

Kahn-Egan, S. (1998). Pedagogy of the pissed: Punk pedagogy in the first-year writing classroom. *College Composition and Communication, 49*(1), 99–104.

Karpp, L. (2019). Queer (-/and) feminist DIY practices in punk and the 'sexual turn' in human rights. *Forum for Inter-American research* (FIAR), *12*(2), 15–36.

Kelly, P. (2006). The entrepreneurial self and 'youth at-risk': Exploring the horizons of identity in the twenty-first century. *Journal of Youth Studies, 9*(1), 17–32.

Kreider, S. E. (2022). Anarchy in aesthetics. In Heter, J. & Greene, R. (Eds.). *Punk rock and philosophy: Research and destroy* (pp. 289–296). LaSalle: Carus Books.

Kwiatek, T. (2022). The essence of punk. In Heter, J. & Greene, R. (Eds.). *Punk rock and philosophy: Research and destroy* (pp. 3–10). LaSalle: Carus Books.

Ladson-Billings, G. (1995). Toward a theory of culturally relevant pedagogy. *American Educational Research Journal, 32*(3), 465–491.

Ladson-Billings, G. (2009). *The dreamkeepers: Successful teachers of African American children* (2nd ed.). San Francisco: Wiley.

Ladson-Billings, G. (2014). Culturally relevant pedagogy 2.0: a.k.a. the remix. *Harvard Educational Review, 84*(1), 74–84.

Ladson-Billings, G. (2018). From Big Homie the O.G. to GLB: Hip-hop and the reinvention of a pedagogue. In Emdin, C. & Adjapong, E. (Eds). *# HipHopEd: The compilation on hip-hop education* (pp. 21–26). Leiden: Brill.

Lee, C., Nasir, N., Pea, R. & De Royson, M. (2020). Introduction: Reconceptualising learning – A critical task for knowledge-building and teaching. In Nasir, N., Lee, C. Pea, R. & De Royston, M. (Eds). *Handbook of the cultural foundations of learning* (pp. xvii-xxxv). New York: Routledge.

Lee, H. (2017). The political economy of 'creative industries'. *Media, Culture & Society, 39*(7), 1078–1088.

Lesko, N. (2012). *Act your age! A cultural construction of adolescence* (2nd ed.). New York: Routledge.

Lindgren, T. (2020). The figuration of the posthuman child. *Discourse: Studies in the Cultural Politics of Education, 41*(6), 914–925.

Linklater, R. (Director). (2003). *School of Rock* (Motion Picture). United States: Paramount Pictures.

Love, B. (2014). Urban storytelling: How storyboarding, moviemaking, and hip-hop based education can promote students' critical voice.*English Journal, 103*(5), 53–58.

Lusty, N. (2017). Riot grrrl manifestos and radical vernacular feminism. *Australian Feminist Studies, 32*(93), 219–239.

Martin, A. J., & Collie, R. J. (2019). Teacher–student relationships and students' engagement in high school: Does the number of negative and positive relationships with teachers matter? *Journal of Educational Psychology, 111* (5), 861–876.

Mayes, E., Keddie, A., Moss, J., Rawolle, S., Paatsch, L. & Kelly, M. (2019). Rethinking inequalities between deindustrialisation, schools and educational research in Geelong. *Educational Philosophy and Theory, 51*(4), 391–403.

Mignolo, W. (2007). Introduction: Coloniality of power and de-colonial thinking. *Cultural Studies, 21*(2–3), 155–167.

Mignolo, W. (2023). The colonial matrix of power. In Christiansen, C., Machado-Guichon, M., Mercader, S., Hunt, O. & Jha, P. (Eds.). Talking about global inequality: Personal experiences and historical perspectives (pp. 39–46). Cham: Palgrave Macmillan.

McInerney, D., Walker, R. & Liem, A. (Eds.). (2011). *Sociocultural theories of learning and motivation: Looking back, looking forward.* Charlotte: Information Age.

McLaren, P. & Scatamburlo-D'Annibale, V. (2004). Paul Willis, class consciousness, and critical pedagogy. In Dolby, N., Dimitriadis, G. & Willis, P. (Eds.). *Learning to labor in new times* (pp. 35–51). New York: Routledge.

Moll, L., Amanti, C., Neff, D. & Gonzalez, N. (1992). Funds of knowledge for teaching: Using a qualitative approach to connect homes and classrooms. *Theory Into Practice, 31*(2), 132–141.

Mooney, M., Dobia, B., Barker, K., Power, A., Watson, K. & Yeung, A. (2008). *Positive behaviour for learning: Investigating the transfer of a United States system into the New South Wales Department of Education and Training Western Sydney Region schools.* Penrith: University of Western Sydney.

More, R. (2004). Postmodernism and punk subculture: Authenticity and deconstruction. *Communication Review, 7*(3), 305–327.

Morrison, A., Rigney, L. I., Hattam, R. & Diplock, A. (2019). *Toward an Australian culturally responsive pedagogy: A narrative review of the literature.* Adelaide: University of Adelaide.

Neimanis, A. & McLachlan, L. (2022). Composting (in) the gender studies classroom: Growing feminisms for climate changing pedagogies. *Curriculum Inquiry, 52*(2), 218–234.

Newsinger, J. (2015). A cultural shock doctrine? Austerity, the neoliberal state and the creative industries discourse. *Media, Culture & Society, 37*(2), 302–313.

Nguyen, M. (2012). Riot grrrl, race and revival. *Women & Performance: A journal of feminist theory, 22*(2), 173–196.

Norton, B. (2017). Thin green line: Environmental politics and punk music. *Ecomusicology Review*. Retrieved from https://ecomusicology.info/thin-green-line-environmental-politics-and-punk-music/.

Nxumalo, F., Nayak, P. & Tuck, E. (2022). Education and ecological precarity: Pedagogical, curricular, and conceptual provocations. *Curriculum Inquiry, 52*(2), 97–107.

Nxumalo, F. & Vintimilla, C. D. (2020). Explorations of the tensions and potentials of de-centering the human in early childhood education research. *Equity & Excellence in Education, 53*(3), 271–275.

Paris, D. (2012). Culturally sustaining pedagogy: A needed change in stance, terminology and practice. *Educational Researcher, 41*(3), 93–97.

Parkinson, T. (2017). Being punk in higher education: Subcultural strategies for academic practice. *Teaching in Higher Education, 22*(2), 143–157.

Parkinson, T. (2018). Being punk in higher education: Subcultural strategies for academic practice. In Smith, G., Dines, M. & Parkinson, T. (Eds.). *Punk pedagogies: Music, culture and learning* (pp. 173-190). New York: Routledge.

Pinar, W. (2019). *What is curriculum theory* (3rd ed.). New York: Routledge.

Reid, A. (2020). *Changing Australian education: How policy is taking us backwards and what can be done about it*. Abingdon: Routledge.

Reles, S. & Clemens, R. (2018). 'Do it yourself' scholarship: From punk rock to qualitative research. *International Journal of Qualitative Studies in Education, 31*(4), 312–327.

Riddle, S. & Apple, M. (2019). Education and democracy in dangerous times. In Riddle, S. & Apple, M. (Eds.). *Re-imagining education for democracy* (pp. 1–10). Abingdon: Routledge.

Rizvi, F. (2022). Education and the politics of anti-globalization. In Rizvi, F., Lingard, B. & Rinne, R. (Eds.), *Reimagining globalization and education* (pp. 214–227). New York: Routledge.

Romero, N. (2016). The new culture wars in ethnic studies. In Sandoval, D., Buenavista, T., Marin, J. & Ratcliff, A. (Eds.). *Rise above: Filipina/o-American studies and punk rock pedagogy* (pp. 117–133). Santa Barbara: Praeger.

Romero, N. (2021). Punx up, bros down: Defending free speech through punk rock pedagogy. *Educational Philosophy & Theory, 53*(11), 1063–1073.

Romero, N., Estellés, M. & Grant, W. (2023). Theorizing Māori–Philippine solidarities through agential realism and punk rock pedagogy. *Research in Education, 115*(1), 47–63.

Said, E. (2019 [1978]). *Orientalism*. London: Penguin.

Sandlin, J. & McLaren, P. (2010). Introduction: Exploring consumption's pedagogy and envisioning a critical pedagogy of consumption – living and learning in the shadow of the 'shopocalypse'". In Sandlin, J. & McLaren, P. (Eds.). *Critical pedagogies of consumption: Living and learning in the shadow of the 'shopocalypse'* (pp. 1–19). New York: Routledge.

Santos, T. & Guerra, P. (2018). From punk ethics to the pedagogy of the *Bad Kids*: Core values and social liberation. In Smith, G., Dines, M. & Parkinson, T. (Eds.). *Punk pedagogies: Music, culture and learning* (pp. 210–224). New York: Routledge.

Scarlett, W. G. (Ed.). *The Sage encyclopedia of classroom management.* London: Sage.

Schilt, K. & Giffort, D. (2012). 'Strong riot women' and the continuity of feminist subcultural participation. In Bennett, A. & Hodkinson, P. (Eds.). *Aging and youth cultures: Music, style and identity* (pp. 146–158). London: Berg.

Schwartz, J. (2015). Listening in circles: Punk pedagogy and the decline of western music education. *Punk & Post-punk*, 4(2–3), 141–157.

Schwartz, J. & Robertson, S. (2018). Laughing all the way to the stage: Pedagogies of comedic dissidence in punk and hip-hop. In Smith, G., Dines, M. & Parkinson, T. (Eds.). *Punk pedagogies: Music, culture and learning* (pp. 128–143). New York: Routledge.

Silva, A. & Guerra, P. (2019). The global and local music scenes: The multiple anchoring of Portuguese punk. In Bestley, R., Dines, M., Gordon, A. & Guerra, P. (Eds.). *The punk reader: Research transmissions from the local and the global* (pp. 69–95). Bristol: Intellect.

Smith, G. (2018). 'There's only one way of life, and that's your own'. In Smith, G., Dines, M. & Parkinson, T. (Eds.). *Punk pedagogies: Music, culture and learning* (pp. 191–209). New York: Routledge.

Smith, G. (2020). Rap, racism and punk pedagogy. In Kallio, A. (Ed.). *Difference and division in music education* (pp. 108–127). New York: Routledge.

Smith, G., Dines, M. & Parkinson, T. (2018). Presenting punk pedagogies in practice. In Smith, G., Dines, M. & Parkinson, T. (Eds.). *Punk pedagogies: Music, culture and learning* (pp. 1–10). New York: Routledge.

Snaza, N. & Weaver, J. (2014). Introduction: Education and the posthumanist turn. In Snaza, N. & Weaver, J. (Eds.). *Posthumanism and educational research* (pp. 1–14). New York: Routledge.

Spring, J. (2010). Schooling for consumption. In Sandlin, J. & McLaren, P. (Eds.). *Critical pedagogies of consumption: Living and learning in the shadow of the 'shopocalypse'* (pp. 69–82). New York: Routledge.

Soutphommasane, T. & Low, R. (2023). Tomorrow's Australia: Race and racialization in Australian education. In Scott, J. & Bajaj, M. (Eds.). *World yearbook of education 2023: Racialization and educational inequality in global perspective* (pp. 119–138). Abingdon: Routledge.

Stafford, A. (2014). *Pig city: From the Saints to Savage Garden.* St Lucia: University of Queensland Press.

Steward, T. (2019). 'We just make music': Deconstructing notions of authenticity in the Iranian DIY underground. In Bestley, R., Dines, M., Gordon, A. & Guerra, P. (Eds.). *The punk reader: Research transmissions from the local and the global* (pp. 229–247). Bristol: Intellect.

Stewart, F. & Way, L. (2023). Introduction. In Stewart. F. & Way, L. (Eds). *Punk pedagogies in practice: Disruptions and connections* (pp. xi–xxii). Bristol: Intellect.

Sugarcubes. (1997). Moby: *Animal Rights* (album review). Retrieved 10 October 2023 from www.sputnikmusic.com/review/75336/Moby-Animal-Rights/.

Taylor, A. (2020). Countering the conceits of the Anthropos: Scaling down and researching with minor players. *Discourse: Studies in the Cultural Politics of Education, 41*(3), 340–358.

Tomlinson, C. (2017). *How to differentiate instruction in academically diverse classrooms* (3rd ed.). Alexandria: ASCD.

Torrez, E. (2012). Punk pedagogy: Education for liberation and love. In Furness, Z. (Ed.). *Punkademics: The basement show in the ivory tower* (pp. 131–142). Brooklyn: Autonomedia.

Tuck, E. & Yang, W. (2014). Introduction to youth resistance research and theories of change. In Tuck, E. & Yang, W. (Eds.). *Youth resistance research and theories of change* (pp. 1–23). New York: Routledge.

van Dermijnsbrugge, E. (2023). Imagining alternative futures in the present: Punk ethnography as a futures forming practice in education and beyond. In Stewart. F. & Way, L. (Eds.). *Punk pedagogies in practice: Disruptions and connections* (pp. 7–26). Bristol: Intellect.

Vass, G. (2016)..Everyday race-making pedagogies in the classroom. *British Journal of Sociology of Education. 37*(3), 371–388.

Vass, G. (2017). Getting inside the insider researcher: Does race-symmetry help or hinder research? *International Journal of Research and Method in Education, 40*(2), 137–153.

Vass, G. (2023). Punk teacher education: Finding ways to interrupt the harmful effects of teacher accountabilities. *Research in Education, 115*(1), 29–46.

Watkins, M. & Noble, G. (2019). Lazy multiculturalism: Cultural essentialism and the persistence of the Multicultural Day in Australian schools. *Ethnography and Education, 14*(3), 295–310.

Way, L. (2021). Punk is just a state of mind: Exploring what punk means to older punk women. *Sociological Review, 69*(1), 107–122.

Webster, S. & Ryan, A. (2019). *Understanding curriculum: The Australian context* (2nd ed.). New York: Cambridge University Press.

West-Newman, C. & Sullivan, M. (2013). Becoming identities. In Matthewman, S., West-Newman, C. & Curtis, B. (Eds.). *Being sociological* (2nd ed., pp. 101–119). Basingstoke: Palgrave Macmillan.

Wolfe, P. (2016). *Traces of history: Elementary structures of race.* New York: Verso.

Woods, M. (2022). Decolonization, decolonial excess, and punk: Reflections on the cultural politics of race and coloniality in North Atlantic punk. *Cultural Studies, 36*(4), 519–542.

Woods, P. (2021). The aesthetic pedagogies of DIY music. *Review of Education, Pedagogy and Cultural Studies, 43*(4), 338–357).

Xiao, J. (2019). The punk subculture in China. In Bestley, R., Dines, M., Gordon, A. & Guerra, P. (Eds.). *The punk reader: Research transmissions from the local and the global* (pp. 293–309). Bristol: Intellect.

Zemblyas, M. (2020). The affective modes of right-wing populism: Trump pedagogy and lessons for democratic education. *Studies in Philosophy and Education, 39*, 151–166.

Acknowledgements

I would like to thank my good friends who – over more years than seem possible – have shared so many memorable nights in and out, listening to music, chatting about music, and getting lost in music. The banter, politics and navel-gazing has been fun too! This collection of ruminations in written form would not have been possible without your provocations, laughs, and irreverence.

Cambridge Elements ≡

Critical Issues in Teacher Education

Tony Loughland
University of New South Wales

Tony Loughland is an Associate Professor in the School of Education at the University of New South Wales, Australia. Tony is currently leading projects on using AI for citizens' informed participation in urban development, the provision of staffing for rural and remote areas in NSW, and on Graduate Ready Schools.

Andy Gao
University of New South Wales

Andy Gao is a Professor in the School of Education at the University of New South Wales, Australia. He edits various internationally renowned journals, such as *International Review of Applied Linguistics in Language Teaching* for De Gruyter and *Asia Pacific Education Researcher* for Springer.

Hoa T. M. Nguyen
University of New South Wales

Hoa T. M. Nguyen is an Associate Professor in the School of Education at the University of New South Wales, Australia. She specializes in teacher education/development, mentoring and sociocultural theory.

About the Series
This series addresses the critical issues teacher educators and teachers are engaged with in the increasingly complex profession of teaching. These issues reside in teachers' response to broader social, cultural, and political shifts and the need for teachers' professional education to equip them to teach culturally and linguistically diverse students.

Cambridge Elements ☰

Critical Issues in Teacher Education

Elements in the Series

Printed in the United States
by Baker & Taylor Publisher Services